Thank you poetry!
Shilpa

Inside the
Medicine Buddha

Life, Tibetans, and My Summer in Nepal

Shilpa Kamat

PublishAmerica

Baltimore

© 2002 by Shilpa Kamat.

First printing

ISBN: 1-59129-409-6
PUBLISHED BY PUBLISHAMERICA BOOK
PUBLISHERS
www.publishamerica.com
Baltimore

Printed in the United States of America

this book is dedicated
to good listeners
and all the poets in the world, fluid or repressed
for everyone who stands up for without wrenching down with
for parents, especially mine
for sisters, especially mine
for insomniacs, just because

Introduction and Acknowledgements

"It sounds like magic," Casey said. She was seven and looking through the stack of pictures from Nepal. I had described to her the way that traditional Tibetan doctors examine their patients.

I jumped into a defensive explanation of how the doctors' methods are really science, rambled, trailed off. I knew that my explanation was lost on her, and in any case, she didn't care about the distinction, was happier to consider it magic. Besides, she might as well have said that about half the people Namrata and I interviewed—they sound like magic to me as I write about them. When it comes to their stories, I know that most readers will share Casey's reaction.

So this is the part of the book where I declare that no matter how fantastic any of the events or stories to follow might seem, to the people involved, to the people around them, they are absolutely true. More than that—they are matter-of-fact, ordinary.

I perpetually find the ordinary amazing.

I have kept the information conveyed through translation as accurate as I could. Bear in mind that hearing a story in translation can be like reading subtitles in a foreign film; a little something is always lost, no matter how good the translation.

For the sake of readers like me who like to say words in their heads as they read them, and for Namrata's sake: "num-ruh-tha" is how her name is pronounced, if you don't know. Just like that, equal emphasis on all the syllables. You'll read it a lot in the book.

Finally, I extend a round of thank yous for the deserving:

To my research partner, Namrata Shah, for her painfully strong work drive and for being a good friend;

To members of the Carleton faculty and student body who supported us in the fellowship proposal process;

To Richard Salisbury, for creating the fellowship in the first place;

To our translator, Ngodup Tsering, for his thoroughness and for introducing us to so many fascinating individuals;

To my family, both immediate and extended, for their support;

To everyone we interviewed, in this book or not;

To those who gave me feedback on my manuscript, especially Priya, Neeta, Mollie, and Namrata;

To you for reading;

And to everyone who e-mailed me frequently while I was abroad for making me feel connected to the rest of the world and helping me through the more difficult days.

Prologue: The Researchers Becoming

When Namrata and I reunited at the airport in Delhi, ready for our connection to Katmandu, we could not stop talking. Our thoughts spilled endlessly into each other's ears and into the ears of the people around us as we waited in plastic airport chairs and stood in long security lines. Her flight from Chicago had reached town the night before; I had flown in the day before from Mumbai, where I had stayed with relatives for three weeks after a term abroad in London. Namrata and I had not seen each other since winter term at Carleton College, when we concocted our project.

The project had started with the first overlap, the desire to learn with the desire to travel. Then her will overlapped mine. Nepal, we decided, and searched for more overlaps, negotiated my interests and hers, the timeframe, parental concerns, the benefits of one area of the country over another. Most of all, we needed a topic.

Traditional medicine, we decided. Namrata's on the medical track, and it interested her, the holistic approach. I cloak myself with the holistic approach, and like her, I wanted to go to a country where herbal remedies are as mainstream as antibiotics. To talk to traditional doctors and their patients, to study the role that the mind plays in healing.

She wanted to learn their methods and how they work. I wanted to learn their stories and share them with others. Namrata and I were decided.

After that, all we had to do was build a plan solid enough to withstand the scrutiny of the board of administrators allocating the fellowships.

*

Namrata and I met on the first day of New Student Week at Carleton. Our parents spotted one another in Burton Dining Hall, happy to see other Indians. They introduced us to one another as we faced awkwardly, somewhere between the salad bar and spaghetti lines.

Initially, our similar ethnic background was the point of interest that drew us together again. There are not very many South Asians at the college, and we wanted to organize cultural activities. So we talked some more, and I bewildered her, and over the course of the year we became friends. Combining our energies, we initiated various South Asian Society events and discovered in the process that we work well together.

Some of the things we found out in between: Her family speaks Gujrati and mine speaks Konkani. She grew up in Chicago and so has a distinctive Chicago accent. My family moved to the US from London when I was seven and bounced around to various states, so I have a mutant accent (though slurred enough that my grandfather informed me, "You don't speak English. You speak American.").

The most objective statement I can make about Namrata's character: she is ruthlessly honest. When it comes to work, she is ultra-conscientious and I keep perspective. When it comes to people, I am ultra-sensitive and she is tougher. I think she takes the practicalities of life too seriously. She thinks I take people too seriously. We are both right.

During fall term of our third year as we ate bagel sandwiches, Namrata suggested applying for a fellowship. Books and maps and hours and five drafts of application led to the day in March when we jumped up and down on the pavement, the congratulatory letter between us.

I: One Day

Tibetans have no fear of heights. The Nepali population in general seems quite unconcerned with the dangers of placing chairs on the edges of rooftops. Children hang precariously from trees, nonchalant and good-humored. Babies stand in windows observing the world several stories below.

The monastery was no exception, fearlessly constructed without a banister on the steps leading up to the cement rooftop. On the roof, no barriers obscured our view of the valley...

"July 1, 2000," blue ink bled into my journal around four in an afternoon promising to be typical and empty. Namrata was jittery, frustrated by the fact that time in Nepal lags lazily behind the racing secondhand of a clock. She works on extremes, she told me, so if she could not be a workaholic, she would fall into vacation mode and not want to do anything at all.

The latter was all right with me. I found the slower pace of life a welcome change from the choppy attention span of the States. In this part of the world, I could take my time talking and eating and be considered typical rather than inefficient. I shared Namrata's concern about our research—we had barely spoken to anyone about traditional medicine and needed a focus. But I knew that trying too hard would only blind me to possibilities when they arose. *Relax, flow with your surroundings*, I told myself as I had told her.

Instead, I realized how much I wanted to break away from my surroundings. We had been in Nepal for nearly a week, and I had seen nothing but metropolis. When we were landing in Katmandu, its sight had thrilled us as our plane sifted through clouds to reveal the fertile green contours of the valley. Life on the ground did not prove so inspiring. For the first three days, I had choked on dust and fumes in the tourist trap of Thamel, where the only natural thing in sight was sky. We had finally moved out to Bodhnath, where I breathed a bit more easily and feasted on the view of the faraway mountains from our hotel room. The hills were tantalizing as ripe watermelons, and I could not stand the drabness of civilization anymore; I wanted out.

Namrata wanted a nap.

Knowing my research partner, I was quite aware that "Let's go for a hike up steep hills that will make you huff and puff so we can commune with nature even though it's the middle of the afternoon" would not go over well. I searched wildly in the guidebook for a target, for something that would make it worth the trip for her…and my eyes rolled across an idea. I announced it to Namrata as she lay sprawled across the bed, succumbing to the lethargy of the Nepali summer day. First, a visit to the Kopan Monastery, where we could ask about traditional doctors who we might be able to talk to, and then a lovely long stroll from there to Gokarna, where a Shiva temple sits at the edge of the Bhagmati River, centuries-old carvings of various gods surrounding it.

If nothing else, the suggestion of furthering our research sold her.

Less enthused about walking up steep hills than I was, Namrata insisted on our taking a taxi up to the monastery. I enjoyed looking out as the driver twisted higher and higher on winding valley roads, and as we crossed over the muddier parts, I was rather happy to have come up in the cab myself. Even so, as we approached the monastery, I turned to Namrata. "See, this isn't as far as that lady told us. We could have had a nice walk…"

The monastery at Kopan is the most touristy one around, offering meditation classes to foreigners. There were presently none being taught; not many people travel during the monsoon. When we asked if someone might be able to tell us about Tibetan medicine, the monk in the main office replied that he would introduce us to a Sister when she was free in another half-hour. He encouraged us to explore while we waited, so after visiting the temple and glancing into the closed library, we settled contentedly on the roof. Veiled by a thin mist, the hills around us seemed like a setting in a Hindi movie. We could hear only the cries of birds where we sat, glancing through the pamphlet we had been given. I thought of what a blissful life the monks and nuns must have compared to the villagers we observed on our way up as they toiled in the sun.

We interviewed Ani Karin at teatime. She invited us to drink Jasmine tea with her in the cafeteria. I imagine I burned my tongue as always, but I remember only how much our conversation energized me over the warmth of the tea as rain splattered outside.

"I joined a monastery twenty-four years ago," Ani Karin told us. Originally from Sweden, she traveled to Nepal and bumped into the Four Noble Truths. She spoke of how real they seemed to her, how enlightening—of how Tibetan Buddhism seeped in and filled a void in her life.

She was nervous when, months later, she spoke to her parents about her wish to become a nun. Her father was taken aback, but she realized that his main concern was how she would support herself. As it turned out, he wound up sponsoring her for a year, and she wound up loving the cloistered life...

But in 1993, she contracted Hepatitis A. (It was something she ate.) Fearing for her life, she went to several doctors, both traditional and allopathic (i.e. schooled in Western medicine) for treatment. It struck me to hear a Buddhist nun speak of her fear of dying, reminding me that no matter how much a person might accept the notion that life is transient, facing death is never easy. However, Tibetan medicine cured her. She remembers how a doctor, seventy years old, examined her. She was scared as she lay down on his table, but Ani Karin insists, "He was very personal"—he did not feel like a stranger. He was sensitive to her fears; she looked forward to visiting him and trusted he would make her well.

She called what she felt with the doctor a "karmic connection" that must exist for healing to progress, for medicine to work. As I understood it, this connection is the feeling that a patient gets that the doctor she goes to is meant for her, that this doctor will cure her. It does not have to be with a traditional physician necessarily, she explained. She has felt a karmic connection with allopathic doctors as well. But she admitted that she prefers the subtlety of Tibetan medicine; Tibetan physicians, she explained, catch diseases before they grow serious rather than having to wait and examine symptoms once an ailment is full-blown like Western doctors often do. And medicine is just one part of healing. Tibetan doctors give their patients life advice, from environmental conditions to diet. And they do not charge examination fees. Patients must pay only for their medicine, which is relatively cheap.

After all her praise of Tibetan medicine, Namrata and I perked up when Ani Karin named Dr. Choekyi as another doctor with whom she feels a karmic connection. We had discovered Dr. Choekyi's office ourselves as we wandered across the street from the Bodhnath *stupa*. Namrata noted that we had arranged an interview with her the day before, explained that we were living in a hotel near the *stupa*. Smiling, Ani Karin told us how she enjoys staying at Kopan largely because the monastery is close to the *stupa* at Bodhnath. It is a wish-fulfilling *stupa*, she explained. Or so Tibetan Buddhists all over Nepal call it, the largest *stupa* in Nepal.

Of course, it only grants immaterial wishes, she added, although there are certainly people praying for their Visas to come through. It touched me to hear her relate how she prays as she walks around it, how in the end, her eyes closed, she imagines the *stupa* turning to a cloud of snowflakes that fall around her.

When we left the monastery, the rain had stopped. We trailed down the slightly muddy path running along several hills. But we were not sure where the path to Gokarna started. We asked a group of people laughing in an open shack of a restaurant, and a man about our age with kind brown eyes showed us the way. We thanked him as he left and stood for a moment on the trail, which ran along the edge of the hill high above the village. Looking down, I felt open and alive. Rice paddies, bamboo groves, and forest spread before us, stark and green with rain. Even a rainbow bent over backwards into view.

As we sauntered halfway down the hill to the main trail, stopping to take pictures, we saw that the man had returned behind us…with about seventeen other men. They called to us and started toward us. We did not take our time walking down to the main trail anymore; I descended in an instant, and waited for Namrata, who climbed down more carefully. We walked quickly for a few minutes to be on the safe side, then relaxed. It was still a beautiful day, and I was ecstatic to be surrounded by plants and earth. We stopped and explored an abandoned ruin of a house for one or two minutes. But the sun was going down, and although we passed villagers and other walkers here and there, we didn't want to be walking on the trail alone after dark.

"*Gokarna kaha?*" I asked one man whom we passed.

"Just keep following this road," he responded in English

By the time we reached Gokarna, the sun had set; the temple waited quietly beside the river. Standing on the edge of the Bhagmati in the evening light, we looked at the temple's silhouette against navy sky, crown and trident at the top. We saw a *Shivalinga* in a small shrine, a hollow tree wrapping around to form three of its walls. The main shrine of the temple was closed, but the courtyard was open, and we paced its expanse observing the carvings of gods and goddesses. Some of them were easy to recognize, Rama and Sita, Ishwar, Durga, curving out from ancient tablets of stone. We stopped at each statue to pray, and I closed my eyes, opening myself to the image, letting it settle into me. That is as explicitly as I can describe prayer for me, an opening and settling.

As we walked through the courtyard, a monkey prowled about, leaping from carving to carving. When we reached a god on which it perched, its head shot forward in a sudden motion, teeth bared in a hiss, ferocious eyes gleaming wildly. I jumped back, gasping.

An old Indian *sadhu* sat beside the main shrine, his uncut hair and beard flowing gray with age, his ascetics' eyes boring through us. I am always a little frightened of *sadhus*, of their unsmiling intensity, but this one talked to us as we passed him, and his conversation put me at ease. He asked if we were Indian, and Namrata spoke with him in Hindi, explaining that we were students researching. He pointed to the statues visible through the mesh around a closed section of the temple; "*Shivaji*," he pointed, and named a few other gods including some we did not recognize, probably variations of Shiva.

There were some young men hanging out at the shrine at this point, some of them only boys but some older; as we walked around the temple, examining the gracefully elongated figures of Parvati and Lakshmi along the roof, their disruption made us decide that it was time to go.

We left from the entrance since we had come in from behind the courtyard; in the increasing darkness as evening set in, we could barely make out the statues leading out, Ganpati, Saraswati. The young Buddha meditated at the end, which is really the beginning, shut-eyed and tranquil.

We could not determine which bus would take us back the way we needed to go, so we began walking down ourselves, the stars of more and more electric lights revealing themselves below as we descended. "Civilization!" Namrata proclaimed, delighted. She is such a city girl. Villagers walked the street as well, on their way home; Namrata and I avoided stepping under streetlights, and I attempted to walk in a manly stagger. Our relatives had insisted on the unsafeness of walking about at night; we weren't taking any chances. Halfway down, we came across a cab driver as he reached home from the day's work. We asked for a ride down, and he obliged, and suddenly, we were speeding along. The upbeat Nepali folk songs blaring from the radio made me happy; most cab drivers did not play music.

He dropped us off at the entrance to the *stupa*. We never did figure out how to direct taxis to our hotel; we were used to entering the square where the *stupa* towered above us and finding our way through back alleys. We were not overeager to do this at night, especially since we saw no other women on the street, but we did not have a choice. In any case, we were hungry, so we crossed the street for dinner at the restaurant of Hotel Tibet, a rather classy place whose chef loved ginger—every meal that we ordered there contained large amounts. When we could put it off no longer, we braved the back streets at night for the first time; a few wrong turns and some backtracking later, we reentered our hotel, deciding that our families might have made us a tad too paranoid.

We stopped next door to our room to let Sara and Brad know that we had returned safely. They were also Carleton students and had been in Nepal since the beginning of the summer. They played many card games to pass the time, and Sara had become particularly obsessed with Spades. As usual, she and Brad sucked us into a game until late in the night. I felt impatient for the game to end, ready to get back to my journal to capture the afternoon's experiences.

For me, breakthroughs are always spontaneous. I find that when I move through events without trying too hard to force things one way or another, everything falls into place.

The day was somewhat contrived, of course; human life always is. Namrata and I had started our morning with a yoga session. At the Pema Lamo Hotel, we were surrounded by Tibetan Buddhist monasteries. The chanting of monks sifted through our screened windows as we awoke each morning, and "Christmas lights" glowed brightly around curving rooftops at night. As I fell into the dead man's position, I incorporated the chanting into my meditation, the horn reverberating in my mind, the drumbeats far more soothing than the hammering and drilling of construction workers below.

True to our refined schedule, we plodded down the steps of our hotel into the burning sunlight. We walked through the green boundaries of our hotel, shuffling down the dusty street already crowded with shopkeepers, vendors, and eager tourists. My nose was not quite so stuffy that it did not twitch when overwhelming gusts of incense-smoke wafted up my nasal passages. Tibetan monks blended into the crowd, marching beside uniformed schoolchildren, passing lounging beggars. It was strange to think that we ate in popular monk hangouts, but hordes of them would enter, laughing and chatting, as we chewed on vegetable *momo*. Little boy monks would play cricket with other boys on the street in front of our hotel. Teenaged monks would call out rowdily as they rode in the back of a pickup truck. I recall a young monk who would strut down the street every day, a pair of sunglasses shading his eyes, whose stance and features reminded Namrata and me of someone we knew in Minnesota; his appearance would send me into peals of laughter.

We bought bananas for our breakfast since we could not eat before doing yoga, handing a third fruit to the grasping hand of a beggar who sat expectantly at our feet. As always, I clasped a bottle of water under my arm. We walked halfway around the monstrous Bodhnath *stupa* and out through the main entrance, down the street and up the stairs, where our waiting teacher bounded enthusiastically into our Nepali lesson; today, we would learn verbs.

I have always been uncomfortable in other-language classes. Whenever I have to speak a language I am not proficient in, my brain drags. My stuttering thoughts block my will to respond, and I always give minimal answers, staying silent until forced to speak.

In a two-person class, a student cannot remain silent for long. Pabitra drilled us thoroughly to ensure that we retained what she taught. Since Nepali is very similar to Hindi, the words slipped easily into our vocabulary—I was just hesitant to let them slip off my tongue, letting Namrata do most of the talking instead. We asked each other about eating breakfast, what we did and didn't do yesterday, our fathers' ages. "*Ramro, ekdam ramro,*" our teacher praised. As I sneezed on chalkdust in the blackboarded room, I thought what a good teacher Pabitra was, of how good it was to be learning something new, of how I should pull my slumping mind out of its comfortable laxity to grasp the world again.

II: Doctor

We sat before Dr. Choekyi's desk, a fourth chair waiting beside her in case a patient dropped in. The doctor impressed us as extremely professional, a quiet woman who emanated an air of assurance and competence. Moments before, Namrata and I had conspired over lunch at Hotel Tibet. As I finished my very gingery *dahl*, I helped Namrata come up with questions that would help us get started. She scrawled them neatly on the gray lines of her yellow-papered notebook. Then we stalked to the doctor's office, walking through the larger pharmaceutical and waiting area with a long counter and many chairs against the wall to enter one of the two smaller examination rooms where she sat.

However, the question-and-answer session provided minimal information. Dr. Choekyi answered our questions quickly, speaking of how she entered medical school in India when she was twenty, earned her degree there after six years of study. She spoke of the twelve pulses she feels to diagnose a patient and of the various places where the herbs for the medicines sold by her office come from. Though we learned the bones of her practice, when it came to more complex questions, it was difficult to convey precisely what we wished to ask in English since the vocabulary for it does not really exist. And, English being her third language, the doctor could not catch our obscure meanings.

Then she examined me.

I mentioned that I had sinus problems, that Ani Karin had recommended her abilities highly. The doctor gestured to her patient's chair, and I slipped onto it. Dr. Choekyi took one arm in each of her hands; three fingers pressed against each wrist, and she read six pulses.

"Your sinuses are not so bad," she told me, which was true—they had not been acting up all that much at the time. But she placed her hand on an area of my stomach. "You have pain here," she said. I glanced at Namrata, who was looking as impressed as I felt. The doctor went on to describe intestinal difficulties precisely like the ones I had been suffering from for a while. She felt the pulse on my neck as well and listened to my heartbeat with her stethoscope.

"Are you going to be in town for the next ten days?" she asked, prescribing medication when I said yes. "Come back and see me when it is over for a checkup."

I handed the prescription to a woman behind the counter outside the room, and she filled a paper bag with small brownish herb balls from the appropriate container. It only cost a dollar or two.

I truly wish that I had taken the medicine; the examination, combined with Ani Karin's description of her experience, convinced me of the soundness of Tibetan medicine. I looked at the small ball-shaped pills and told myself that I would begin taking them the very next day. But I did not take the medication because we decided shortly after our interview that we would not stay in town for two more weeks as we had planned; two days later, we boarded a bus for Pokhara.

III. Basic Necessities

Our first afternoon in Pokhara was not the tranquil pastoral experience that Sara had prepared us for. The monsoon fog obscured the hills and lake, and the mountain range behind it was even more beyond our observation. Cramped and weary from our seven-hour bus ride, we carried our bags down the long driveway of the hotel we would be staying in for a night, rough pebbles strewn unevenly beneath our feet.

The hotel that the man at the travel company had booked for us starkly contrasted the glamorous picture that he had shown us. This did not surprise me at all as I had not trusted the picture, but having had higher expectations, Namrata, Sara, and Brad were furious. While they were not the *worst* accommodations we could have chosen, the rooms were less than adequate. Sara and Brad's toilet did not flush; in our bathroom, water barely came out of the taps. Grimy as we were from our ride in the Swiss Army bus, we resolved to shower on the following day when we found our new hotel. The windows in the room were shoddily screened, and insects were everywhere. Namrata groaned woefully, jumping onto her bed when she saw a cockroach, and begged me to get rid of it. She moaned even more when she realized that the television, the one luxury she had looked forward to, produced mostly snow. We managed to focus on a music channel and took refuge for a few moments nonetheless, watching indistinct actors dance to Punjabi tunes.

The four of us decided to escape the dilapidated hotel for some lunch and to look for a new place as soon as possible. I was just happy to finally be outside the metropolis of Katmandu and closer to the hills. Namrata's sentiments were different: "I want to go back to Katmandu!" she announced within ten minutes of our walking about Lakeside.

Hotel shopping was tedious as we plodded from guesthouse to guesthouse, resort to resort, bargaining down the already reduced off-season prices: "But we're students!" I felt bad at the desperation we aroused in some of the hotel workers as they did their best to create attractive bargains. "Not come back?" one of them asked us as we were leaving, his face expressive as an upset three-year-old's. "We might come back tomorrow," we told him, and I could see that he did not believe us.

Monsoon season in Pokhara, with its enormous lake, is far more intense than in Katmandu. The weather is generally cooler, the rains heavier. It started raining while we were hotel hunting. Rainwater flooded the streets past our ankles, and we sloshed through miserably, cowering under two umbrellas, reluctant to return to our original hotel for the night. Sara and I headed back earlier because she was sick and my allergies had been working up enough to make me tired and weak.

I wanted to visit an Internet café; eating, sleeping, and showering were secondary at this point to the comfort of curling my fingers onto a keyboard and e-mailing. But I would not have my wish; when I attempted to bargain for lower rates at a computer place on the way back, the owner told me that the ludicrously high price of seven *rupees* a minute was uniform throughout Lakeside, perhaps through all of Pokhara. Not wanting e-mail to get too inexpensive, they set a law that keeps anyone running an Internet café from charging any less. I never cared for economics.

The food would not come. I sat at a table in the covered space in the courtyard, Sara and Brad across from me, the rain falling around us making me shiver. They wanted to be away from Nepal and the rain, spoke wishes of fireplaces and other warm things. Their weariness infected me; I was reminded again of how much I needed a break after four months of traveling.

The restaurant workers were busy fussing over a long banquet table of Indian tourists who had pre-ordered a large meal. Our waiter came outside and told me the cheese for the pizza I had ordered was bad. "I didn't want any cheese." I repeated my order, my patience teetering after having waited for forty-five minutes. "Pizza with vegetables and no cheese. And two hot lemons with honey. Can you bring them to my room?" In our present cold-and-wet state, the warm citrus water would serve as a hot chocolate substitute.

Upstairs, Namrata was standing on her bed in her pajamas. "Shilps, there's a cockroach in here," she appealed.

"I don't care," I blurted. I collapsed on my bed, the culmination of all the frustrations my travels had sparked in the past few months imploding in my head. I could not push them back anymore; there was too much empty space from the missing. Namrata turned to me, surprised by my breakdown.

It didn't help that it was another half-hour before the waiter brought the food upstairs on a tray. The spicy brown sauce covering the vegetables repelled my tongue, made it impossible for me to eat. I tried scraping off the sauce, but it was already too much a part of the dish, soaked into the thin crust, marinating the vegetables. I should have just asked for some rice and *dahl*, I thought in retrospect, but I had already eaten a very salty bowl of *dahl* for lunch when the bus stopped at a restaurant on the way.

A hotel worker came by to place a chemical mosquito repellent in the electric socket beside my bed. He seemed nice. Two random girls from the Indian group also opened our door, perhaps confusing our room for theirs. They stood frozen for an instant, hair braided down their backs, then burst into peals of laughter at their mistake. They ran off without a word, seemed unembarrassed.

Moving out of that hotel was as troublesome as moving in. The matron chased us up the stairs, insisting that her hotel was in a prime location with every convenience, that she could lower prices to make it even more attractive... It was hard to feel sorry for her in her desperation when she was so defensive.

Downstairs, a moustached Indian man who looked like he had stepped out of a sleazy nightclub stood next to the reception desk. As we sat waiting for a ride to our new hotel, he towered above us, heavyset, and cocked an eyebrow. "So…you don't like Nepali and Indian culture?" he demanded, for what other reason could we have for leaving the hotel? He put our nerves on edge, never mind that his accusation made no sense. When we gave a polite reason for leaving, he remarked snidely in Nepali to the other workers, "Those *saalis* are lying." Namrata caught the remark and told me, livid.

Our anger lending our departure a huffy air, we left the hotel as disillusioned as when we had entered.

We spent a month in Pokhara. The tourist-centered world of Lakeside was far more contained than sprawling Boddhnath. Our new hotel, Lake Palace, was down the street from the Hotel Mountaintop where Brad and Sara stayed; their hotel was beside the large main street that ran alongside Lake Fewa.

A banyan tree stood in the intersection, its knurled trunk thick as a family. Green leaves and twisted vines hung over the road, roots encased in a large cylinder of earth. Two other banyan trees stood in similar rings along the street.

The street was lined on both sides with shops, restaurants, and hotels. Water buffalo trailed along, driven away from building fronts by proprietors. Taxis abounded, drivers waiting eagerly for foreign faces. Other cars or motorcycles sped by as well, and all four of us complained that when a vehicle passed us, its driver seemed to go out of his way to steer as close to us as he possibly could.

The best part of living in Lakeside was that we could always find a good place to eat. Since the place was teeming with tourists, many restaurants routinely doused their vegetables with iodine and boiled their water. A variety of restaurants lined the streets, Tibetan, Italian, Indian. The only traditional Nepali dish listed on any of the menus was *dahl-bhat*. Though lentils and rice are some of the most economical foods available, *dahl-bhat* was always the most expensive dish in any restaurant since only a tourist would buy it there.

The restaurants we frequented grew used to Namrata's and my unusual requests. "No cheese," the waiter at The Lemon Tree would immediately guess if we ordered lasagna or pizza. "No sugar," the waiter at Tea Time knew whenever we ordered *lassis*. After weeks of eating "outside food," as my family refers to restaurant food when we are in India, I had grown weary of the rich, stomach-churning dishes that most restaurants tend to serve. Namrata and I went on a non-sugar non-cheese non-butter kick. (The last of these was especially easy since neither of us likes butter anyway. Talk of how people in Old Tibet drank cups of melted butter if they could afford to made us gag.) Content on my quest for lighter foods, Koto was one of my favorite restaurants to visit, the good-but-relatively-expensive Japanese place near the end of the street with an enormous glass window facing the lake and healthier "outside food" than anywhere else. Eating there turned me into a walking ad for the place. I loved the utensils there, the simple plates curving neatly. I accepted cup after cup of green tea just to watch it being poured from the ceramic kettle. At Koto, my tofu craving would be fulfilled, and I would place bits of wasabi on the tip of my tongue, clearing my sinuses with its heat as I bit into rolls of vegetarian sushi.

If I ever grew so full that I could not finish a meal, I could easily pack it up and hand it to a beggar without my famine-weary conscience gnawing at me to finishfinishfinish. One night, I held a plastic bag containing half a portion of fried rice that I had not been able to palate wrapped in tinfoil. Completely oblivious to the world around me as I walked, I mistook a boy who encroached upon my peripheral vision as a beggar and handed him the food. He accepted the bag with a quizzical smile, and I walked on, still out of it until Sara asked me whether I had just handed my food to the boy who was hailing a taxi. "Probably some merchant's kid," Brad commented. I realized how accustomed I was to the small boys recruited to pester tourists on the streets of Lakeside, putting on a cute act for considerable amounts of change.

Our hotel had a restaurant as well, but we tended not to eat there;

many of the foods we wanted were not available during the monsoon, and we liked the change of scenery that searching for restaurants in town gave us. We acquainted ourselves with several staff members, though. This was easy to do since they talked to us every chance they could, unbusy in the off season. The two main receptionists, Deepak and Santosh, were around our age. Deepak admitted he was 25, but told us it was rude to ask his age because a man likes to feel like a teenager until he is married. He was a student of journalism and political science, a smooth talker. Santosh was also a student, and Namrata helped him with his French once or twice. Once, he started beating Deepak for snatching away a "love letter" he was writing. Another time, we walked down the large marble flight of stairs as the two were having a mango-eating competition. Whoever could finish his kilo of mangoes first did not have to pay for them.

Every member of the staff was a man. This created some interesting chemistry, especially since Namrata and I were nearly the only guests staying in the hotel. For instance, there was the visiting manager who played the chivalrous role. He seemed especially interested in pursuing Namrata's heart. "I wonder if I should tell him I have a boyfriend," she mused. He made two "dates" to take us to see *Refugee*, a popular Hindi film playing nearby, and stood us up both times. He stayed at the hotel for a week, though initially he had announced he would be leaving in two days. "Don't be scared—I am here!" he announced once when I opened the door to try catching whoever had been playing with the doorknob. It was most likely either the two-year-old down the hall or one of the drunken men in the room across from us. The visiting manager was the only one who stood in the hall when I opened it, though, and Namrata and I cracked up at his heroics after he left.

One night, when I was taking a shower, I heard Namrata scream. "There's a rat in here!" she called. She had jumped onto her bed and had no intention of stepping down.

"Reach over and call reception," I told her, wanting to finish my shower. I waited in the bathroom as every man on the staff outside barged into the room laughing and cornered the rat, taking it out in a garbage can.

At night, the rat returned, and I woke up just as I was falling asleep to Namrata's shriek at the rustling plastic bag and a shrill squeaking. Namrata went outside and woke the night watchman. He started cursing at her under his breath in Nepali but smiled and asked how he could help in English. He could not find the rat, though, and he finally went back to sleep in the reception area, still cursing at us under his breath. "He must think we're stupid not to understand that," Namrata commented. Cursing transverses language barriers like nothing else.

His resentment was understandable, though; he was the one who had to do all the grunt work at the hotel. Anytime we or any of the other guests requested a favor of the staff, for our room to be dusted or a missing pillow returned, whoever we were talking to would nod agreeably, then scream his name and tell him to do it. He was the one made to run into the sun and down the street to hail a taxi the time we accepted the receptionist's offer. So at times, he acted out, sour-faced and irrational. "Don't ever call here again!" he told my aunt when her phone call one night woke him up at 9:30. "Maybe we should just stuff the door and not worry about the rat," I suggested. "I don't think it'll do anything to us, do you?"

One day, we handed over our laundry, leaving large bags of it with Deepak at reception. That afternoon, as we returned, a group of staff members stood outside laughing, mocking us like annoying younger brothers might. We realized that their behavior must have to do with our clothing. Well, we decided, it was written that they would wash women's underwear as well as anything else, and they washed the clothes of other guests without a fuss, so we would continue expecting the same.

But aside from being a bunch of overgrown boys now and then, the men of Lake Palace were generally helpful. For one thing, their watching TV in our room while we were away ensured that we would have good reception when we returned and wanted to unwind to some music. For another, Deepak was responsible for our finding the first doctor we interviewed in Pokhara: Dr. Labsang Lama.

Deepak found out for us where he lived and drew a confusing map for our taxi driver. We walked upstairs to the doctor's apartment, uncertain as we stood on the terrace whether we would be welcome or even understood. But the woman who answered the door spoke English and courteously invited us inside.

IV. Another Doctor

We were never able to ascertain whether the woman who translated for us was Dr. Labsang Lama's daughter-in-law or daughter, but after bringing us into the apartment, she just as graciously conducted the question-and-answer session. "From six onward, he is a monk, and then he studied medicine. So...the Chinese invaded Tibet, no? So at that time, he changed to army, because there is very less army, so all the monk became army, and they came to India, and they had sons..."

The doctor himself seemed much more a grandfather now than a monk or a Campa revolutionary. He sat on his bed smiling indulgently, his round face abounding with reassurance that must put his patients at ease. His small grandson was bounding about energetically. The boy was thoroughly amused by Namrata and me, remarking to his mother about how we interjected, "Oh! Oh!" whenever we understood a point. In his place, I think my American mannerisms would amuse me, too.

In the midst of our interview, there was a ring at the door. A group of people entered, two men supporting a woman who seemed barely conscious. They were ushered out to the patio and Namrata and I pointed to them in surprise and asked if we should leave so that the doctor could observe the patient.

And instead, the daughter asked if we would like to observe.

"Is that okay?" We were incredulous, but she assented. We moved to the doorway to make room for the family.

The patient seemed woozy and lethargic as the men carrying her placed her on the floor beside the doctor. She was like a large doll dressed in a plain *salwar*, barely able to hold her head up. She asked for water. Dr. Labsang Lama felt her pulses with three fingers on each wrist, as Dr. Choekyi had felt mine. He exchanged words with her family.

"What exactly happened to the patient?" I asked the daughter, who offered to tell us what was going on.

"The brains—um, pulse, no? Is not working, he says. She suffers from faintness and heart pain—because the blood doesn't go to the brain, so there is very little blood in the brain...so she's not able to speak and she's having breathing problems."

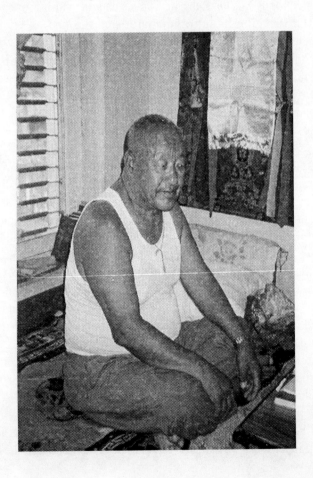

The family explained that the woman had been in her present condition for months. They had just moved to the area and had wanted to bring her to Dr. Lama for some time and were relieved that they were finally granted his expertise.

"If the patient suffers from this, no? If he or she comes immediately, then on that day, the suffering [will be cured] but, uh, they took a long time because they moved here and they didn't find the house..."

It was an exciting experience to watch as Dr. Labsang Lama calmly examined the woman while her relations, his daughter, Namrata, and I hovered about the crowded room, his grandson scampered about, and the blares of car horns and occasional trains reverberated in the apartment. "I could never concentrate in an atmosphere like that," Namrata remarked in admiration as we discussed it later. "I was actually kind of shocked that we were able to see the entire thing..."

The doctor conjectured that the root of the problem was black magic. The daughter explained, "If someone doesn't like her, or if someone is very jealous of them—or her, then they do black magic."

"How did the doctor determine it was black magic?" I asked, fascinated.

"When he checks a person, he know that—whether it is black magic. At the same time, she has um, some blood problems..."

"Oh, I see..." I really didn't, but I realized it would be too difficult to pursue this line of questioning. "So he's giving her medication?"

"Yes."

Sitting in the doorway on the seats that the doctor's grandson brought for us, which I felt vaguely guilty for using while the patient's family sat on the floor, it felt natural to accept that the girl's illness was caused by a jealous curse.

Although she could not tell me how the doctor decided that black magic must be the cause of the illness, the daughter-in-law was able to speculate as to what caused the black magic itself. Besides envious people, there was another possible source: "The goddesses and the gods...because they don't do the prayer regularly sometimes, it affects...Now, he'll give medication and...he'll do some prayers on the patient..." The train drowned out her words.

Dr. Labsang Lama began some sort of ritual. "In Tibet, no, he's a monk, so he know everything," the daughter-in-law explained. "So if he does this prayer, no? The patient will get relief from the black magic."

He began chanting mantras, his tone very calm, voice almost trance-like as he set fire to herbs, fanning the smoke toward the patient with a peacock feather. The older woman holding her, perhaps her mother, grasped the smoking pot and held it close to the younger woman's nose. Dipping the peacock feather into a pot, the doctor sprinkled sacred water on the patient.

Then he poured some of the holy water from the chalice directly into the patient's mouth. Picking up his prayer book, he pressed it against his head as he prayed. He turned to the patient, still chanting, and placed it onto her head, still chanting. Then he smacked it sharply against the back of her head. Again and again, he struck her with the book, as if to exorcize bad spirits while the rest of us watched, transfixed. The woman holding her winced.

He moved the book to her back, holding it there for a moment, his chant still trance-like. He clapped it on her back several times as well. Then he brought out some red thread.

"This is a sacred thread...so with this thread, no? The monks will do prayer, and each will protect the patient from black magic..."

The doctor tied the string around her neck, around her left upper arm. He put a red paper in her mouth and sprinkled more holy water from the pot with the peacock feather. Finally, he blew on her, one breath after another.

The ritual complete, he spoke once again to the family. He handed them medicine to give the girl, and they paid him.

We asked his daughter-in-law where the medicine came from. "In Tibet, previously, they don't have pills—only powder. And in India, after coming to India, because of the climate, the powder is not in good shape—maybe it is decaying because of the climate. Sometimes it's very hot and the powder gets changed. So they changed to the balls. The patients have to chew the balls with the pills—with hot water." These were pills like the ones I had bought at Dr. Choekyi's office. Those ones, my instructions said to dissolve in hot water. After leaving them exposed in that first infested hotel where we stayed for a day, I felt it too unsanitary to consider taking them anymore.

The pills, though, would only help her recover now that the cause of the disease, the black magic, had been expelled. "[Illnesses from black magic] cannot be cured by the doctors. As he's a monk, he does *puja*, and he knows what to do. It's working."

"How frequently do patients come in who've had black magic affecting them?" I asked the daughter-in-law. She did not have exact numbers but told me that many Nepali patients as well as Tibetans seek the doctor's help. "The younger generation often do not believe, but they'll come back if the [allopathic] doctors' medication doesn't work." Labsang Lama always advises his patients not to mix allopathic and traditional medicines.

The patient's family carried her out of the house; the examination and *puja* had taken about twenty minutes. Dr. Lama's wife brought in their two-month-old granddaughter, and he started playing with her contentedly. We could tell it was time for us to make an exit. But Namrata had one last question. She wanted to know if there were women doctors in Tibet.

"Actually, there are, uh, women who [were] studying Tibetan medicine, it seems, but they [were] not practicing it. Before in Tibet. Privately, they [were] practicing. But now, actually, they don't take the pulse and practice as doctors. But there are students—women students...after the invasion, women who were studying Tibetan medicine came to India and got a formal education so that they could practice."

Namrata nodded, and we thanked the doctor and his daughter-in-law, exchanging "*Namaste*"s and pressed-together palms. The grandson followed us out to the terrace, waving goodbye from above as we stepped to the ground.

V. Injury

From: "shilpa k"
Subject: tidings
Date: Thursday, July 13, 2000 10:15 AM

*Well, I'd resolved myself to write postcards for most of my time here,
but it's much easier for me to just type about the events of the day
before yesterday. Because quite a bit happened.*

*The day started out well enough although Namrata and I had to
wake up quite early to meet Sara and Brad for breakfast. We were
palnning on walking over the hill to the Tibetan village, and it wasn't
raining as it had the day before, but by the time we finished breakfast,
it was REALLY hot and humid outside. And after walking down the
street toward the hill, asking some people the way to the village and
getting four different ansers simultaneously, we headed back to our
hotels to take a break and decide what to do. I was feeling rather
sick to my stomach at this point (god, the other people e-mailing
around me are obnoxious—americans, of course) and not up to going
to the village, so when we met with Sara and Brad again, we decided
to go to the stupa instead—that is, Sara, Namrata and I did; Brad
decided to stay home and study Arabic.*

*So Namrata, Sara, and I rented out a boat for the day for a
ridiculously low price. It was so wonderful rowing out into the lake.
I really wished that it wasn't as polluted as it is so that I could jump
into it. We rowed out into the middle of the lake where the fresh air
was SOOOO good to my lungs, which are used to choking on fumes*

and dust in town. It was especially nice to perch up on the very edge of the boat (the boats here are pointed on both sides like canoes but much more stable, so you can sit up on the edge and dangle your feet in the water). When we were far enough away that no one could see us from any of the shores, Sara took off her shirt, and I actually did too, and it was much cooler (I also took turns sharing an umbrella with Namrata—my umbrella may be a pathetic shield in the rain, but it makes a nice parasaul(sp?)). We just drifted for a long time, and I felt very meditative and enjoyed chatting and sharing ginger snaps with Namrata and Sara. I completely blocked Pokhara from my sight, looking only at the valley on three sides, which is absolutely gorgeous.

Well, this was the best part of the day, but we had to move on. After stopping way too far away from the restaurant we were trying to reach (Namrata and I walked up a brook, rice paddies all around us, to ask this guy (who was only wearing a towel, sheesh) driections), Sara and I rowed against the tide like mad to finally reach a place on the side of a hill that looked like a hotel (so had a restaurant). We had a very late lunch there (it was about 4:30 in the afternoon) and just relaxed for a while...I discovered that my arms were a bit sunburned, the first time that's ever happened...

And then we decided to climb up to the stupa. Sara especially was very weary of the idea because she doesn't like hiking up hills (Namrata seemed to have some reservations too), but we started off. I asked a couple of girls working in a field which way the right way

was, and one of them started to lead us. she jumped up onto a wall that was about waist-height, and I wasn't sure about following—but then I realized that she was just crossing right over, so I crossed over too. And so did Sara.

And then Namrata, while jumping down, managed to twist her ankle. She immediately recognized her injury as a sprain since apparently she's had prior experience. Sara announced, "Okay, we're going down," quite determinedly—I'm sure she was quite relieved we weren't going up. Namrata was like, "I can just wait in the boat— you two go up." As if we'd do that. So we helped her down to the boat again, tying our socks around her ankle to try to keep it from swelling, and then Sara and I rowed like mad against the tide all the way back to town.

After taking an overpriced cab to the hotel, all the men there (there aren't any women on the staff at all) fussed over Namrata and called a clinic for us, even telling them that Namrata's Indian so that they wouldn't make us pay some large dollar sum. The doctor there announced that she could just start walking right away, which is the worst advice either of us had ever heard—but the X-ray revealed that it was indeed a sprain and not a fracture. That night, Sara helped me move our stuff one floor down to a room on the second floor which is actually a bit nicer that the one above and has a nice terrace with a table and chairs. Of course, they turned the generator off again (the city's been without electricity for several days, and our hotel can't seem to afford to leave their generator on at all times), so I took a shower by candlelight and tried to make Namrata comfortable.

So that's what's up right now. Namrata's ankle isn't terribly bad— she can limp to the bathroom, and I can help her down the stairs— but she'll not be that active for a while. I'm afraid the inactivity will drive her crazy, so I was suggesting that we take a cab out to someplace other than the hotel where she can sit around and perhaps work on our project during the days. Yesterday, she wasn't doing very well and slept practically all day, but today, Brad, Sara, and I took her out on the lake and paddled her around for awhile (that was cool because there was nearly a storm—maybe I'll write about that in some postcards).

Well, that's basically what I have to report. And look at me, I've been capitalizing sentences today. I'm ready to head back to the hotel and take a shower now—the electricity seems to be back on, and our television actually seems to be working (MTV India's hysterical, and so are its stupid commericials; yesterday on one, this guy was asked, "What do you think about e-mail?" and he replied, "'E-mail'? I think 'female' is better!"). I'll try and write again soon and in any case, I'll be writing postcards...hope things are good and fine in the States...

shilpa

VI. Recuperating

The day after she sprained her ankle, I undertook a short-lived mission to find Namrata crutches. I gave up when I learned how rare they were in the area. But as the doctor had predicted, she was able to walk on her ankle for short distances without straining herself too much. Still, I did not want her to overexert herself, so we took other forms of transportation whenever we could. Lakeside taxi drivers, who routinely inflated prices before, were now incorrigible. They saw Namrata's brace and knew she was helpless. A ride down the street cost us as much as a ride across town.

Namrata worried over her injury more for my sake than her own; she lamented for our research. I did not mind so much myself, but I knew that she would drive both of us crazy if she was cooped up in the hotel as she recovered. I resolved not to let that happen, thinking of ways that we could amuse ourselves that did not require pressing feet on the ground.

One of my favorites was boating. Sara and Brad would pick us up, rowing from the edge of town where we regularly rented boats from a man whose prices were a fourth of what renters in the pier areas beside the hotels charged. The second time we went out with them, it started raining as we drifted toward the center of the lake, as it had on the day I wrote the e-mail. The sky and wind closing around us were as bewitching as the first time, the raindrops when they came spectacular as they forced the lakewater to dance in small straight leaps into the air.

This time, though, we sensed that the brooding clouds would not settle for a brief shower. The waves slapping our boat were growing larger, and all the locals had left the water. Except for a few splashes of color close to Lakeside, we were the only boat in sight. Frantically, Sara and Brad rowed to the narrow strip of land beside a cliff where we could take shelter during the worst of it. We chained the boat against the wildlife just in time. As Sara and Brad huddled under one of their umbrellas, Namrata and I standing close beneath another, the clouds released everything inside them, rain falling like a stampede onto Lake Fewa. I could not stop smiling.

When it settled down as much as we expected it would, we used our empty water bottles to bail as much rainwater as we could from the boat. Sara and Brad started rowing again as Namrata and I continued to bail, the rain still falling though not as heavily as when we were standing beside the cliff. Somehow, they turned the boat toward land without letting the waves knock it over. The whole time, Sara was feeling frantic and I was wildly happy, adrenaline soaring.

One day, Namrata and I jumped in a cab with Sara with the intention of heading up to the *stupa* we had been trying to reach when Namrata sprained her ankle. We planned to lounge around and enjoy the view. "*Goomba?*" the driver asked us when we asked him to drive to the *stupa*, and thinking there was a monastery beside the *stupa*, we nodded. Halfway through the cab ride as we snaked up hillside roads, we saw the *stupa* on the top of a hill far across from us and burst into laughter. The driver, it turned out, was taking us to a monastery on another hill.

Getting out of the taxi, Namrata and I circled a small *stupa*, spinning random prayer wheels on its side as we went around. I sat for a moment on a stone wall, looking down the hill, its vegetation thick and green. Since we were at the monastery, we tried to find someone to talk to about our research. Namrata asked for us in Hindi. One monk said he could introduce us to a healer or something of the sort. I don't remember too well. While we waited, he invited us to come inside the temple as the monks chanted mantras. They sat in two rows facing each other toward the right of the temple. We slipped off our shoes and found empty places on a sheet. I enjoyed their meditation; the drums and voices filled me, and I shifted into the lotus position, closed my eyes, breathed deeply. "Is Shilpa asleep?" Sara whispered to Namrata.

I don't remember why—we left the meditation prematurely and were introduced to a man from the nearby clinic. He led us down the hill, Namrata insisting her ankle was all right as she limped with us, to a house where they made medicine. There was a dog there who looked ill and a woman who we were introduced to, perhaps his wife. The place was a school as well. We followed him upstairs to a room where several small boys and two women were watching a Hindi film on the television in the corner opposite the door. On the counter of the room were hundreds of small herbal pills, prepared and waiting to be bottled. They filled jars on the shelves on the walls behind the television. We snapped pictures with two different cameras, in color and black-and-white film.

VII. Sidetracking

Two staff members of our hotel spoke with us about Nepali and Indian shamans, the *dhami-jakri* faith healers that Namrata was initially interested in focusing on. She had looked through her book on *dhami-jakris* two weeks earlier on the bed of Pema Lamo Hotel in Bodhnath as I flipped through my book on traditional Tibetan medicine, lounging on the mattress on the floor by the window. Dr. Megh Gurung, an allopathic doctor who we had spoken with over lemongrass tea during our first few days in Nepal, had suggested narrowing our focus to just one form of traditional medicine. He recommended the books so that we could do some background research, and we had dutifully bought them from the Pilgrim Bookstore, as well as a *mandala* coloring book and a wooden flute I could not really play.

My book was thin and orange, documenting years of training and successes in healing. Tibetan medicine fascinated me with its focus on the elements and pulses, with its mystic language that could be translated into scientific results. My mind shut off when I skimmed the *dhami-jakri* methods, my intuition shying away from details that did not feel like healing. The *dhami-jakri pujas* felt as fictitious as Presidential debates. "It would be a good study of how the mind affects healing," Namrata insisted. But I wanted to research something that I could believe in, too. I did not want to focus on the shamans.

Convenience favored me; we were surrounded by Tibetans where we were staying. I convinced Namrata that Tibetan medicine was the way to go. But at Lake Palace, with patients of *dhami-jakris* in closer proximity, our research sidled around to Namrata's first choice as we heard about the shamans.

When we interviewed him, Deepak was sitting to the side behind the reception desk. Namrata and I sat in armchairs in front of him. I had asked the cook for a knife so that I could cut a mango upstairs, and he brought it on a porcelain plate, placed it on the desk. In the middle of the interview, Deepak picked it up and started playing with it, pressing the flat sides of the blade against his face, sliding it about. He put it down in a flash when I picked up my camera to take his picture, though.

Deepak's father was a doctor in the army and had a small free clinic in the village; but his *dhami-jakri* uncle holds a far greater status there than an allopathic physician. Unlike the US, in Nepal, non-allopathic healing is mainstream rather than "alternative." Even those who prefer the care of doctors may also consult a shaman. "Many high-quality peoples…they like to go with the famous shaman first… Supposed to make good luck," Deepak explained. However, most people depend primarily on shamans, especially Nepalis living in isolated villages. "[*Dhami-jakris*] are very respected…because they are very kind persons and average peoples believe them, and average people are too far from the…any special doctor." Aside from distance, allopathic doctors are too expensive for the "average" people, so they turn to shamans, who, at least in the village, do not have fixed fees. People can pay a shaman what they can; in the place of money, they can give a hen or a small goat, new clothes, or other things.

Deepak lived for about four years in Bojhpur, a small village in Eastern Nepal. "There are still no telephone, no television, no transports…nothing there. There are people still suffering from many kinds of pains, like human pains…but there are no communications…with any other area…"

"So in this village…are there many *dhami-jakris* there?" Namrata asked.

"Yes, so many," he told us. "And they are very very respected… very very respected…"

"Can you describe them to us?" I asked.

"*Dhami jakri*…there are two kinds of *dhami jakri*, actually. One is...they never wear any kinds of special dress, and they don't have, uh, any fixed state of treatment...They can be anywhere and they can treat themselves anytime. Everywhere, anytime.

"And another one, they are very very special shamans and very respected...they wear a special dress. Some of [them] wear like, white, and some of them wear like, yellow dresses with, uh...[something incomprehensible]...headed cap and ...and many other human bones, and many, many small bells for the music. You know, without drumset, it is not possible to treatment for him." The drums are beaten as the shaman chants himself into a trance.

We asked how the shamans he is familiar with diagnose a patient, and he explained:

"They bury rice in first, in the brass plate, and after, when they chanting themselves, this rice is dancing automatically there in the plate of brass...then shaman able to guess what the problem with person."

"By rice?"

"By rice."

There is a general fear of those who perform black magic, those who possess powers like a shaman's but use them to harm instead of heal. "Witches make bad plans for peoples," Deepak explained. "Can't imagine the shaman without witches." If a witch is responsible for a person's suffering, he told us, only a shaman can help.

When living in Pokhara, Deepak usually goes to an allopathic clinic for medicine if he has a headache or fever, but in September of 1996, he solidified his faith in shamanism when he developed a headache. He tried at first to cure it with allopathic medicine, "but medicine [did] nothing for my health..." His head went on throbbing for hours, so finally, his friends took him to a *dhami* nearby in Pokhara. "...He did something with rice, and he gave me suggestions..." Deepak was made to "eat up something with rice" and to throw a mixture of rice and flour into a stream. "After two days, I...automatically, I feel good," he told us. "I am doing [this] every year, one time in September. Hospitals—medicines—this does nothing for me, and I have to go again."

Deepak's words reinforced for us how thoroughly shamanism is imbedded in Nepali culture, in its spiritual and traditional identity. Although richer families in cities often turn to allopathic doctors for treatment, the spiritual place of shamans transcends class distinctions. "In the Hindu tribes, many people...they respect the shaman...shaman is the number one. One place in Katmandu near Bhaktapur...called Dhuarkurt...there is a Lama there...from western part of Nepal. Our king and queen go monthly there to meet with him... There is no Nepalese society without the shaman," Deepak insisted.

Syed also has been cured by a *dhami* across the border in India. "I was only twelve years old...my mother says 'you have malaria.'" For ten days, he took allopathic medicine, but it was not malaria after all. Finally, he was taken to a *dhami-jakri*. "After four or five days, I was okay," he told us. He remains a skeptic, however. "I believe a little bit in *dhamis*, but not too much," he said.

It was nice to hear about Nepali and Indian shamans, to contextualize the place of the shaman in Nepali society. Interesting, I thought, but I did not expect our interviews with them to have a place in our research. What we did not know was that our interviews with Deepak and Syed were not diverging from our focus as much as we thought; there are also Tibetan shamans. We would be talking to two of them.

VIII. Becoming the Old Shaman

"He says that...uh...he has lots of friends in America. He says that he is very popular in America. Many people know of him, so.... He does not know why you haven't heard of him." Our translator conveys the proud Tibetan shaman's words.

"We are from waaaay in Minnesota. And it's kind of like, um, like a small village in Nepal, so we don't really know—we're not exposed to..." Sara trails off, and our translator relates her answer to the shaman, who seems satisfied with her explanation. We are lucky to have a good translator; our previous one proved painfully inadequate, pushed into the job against his will by friends who insisted that his English was better than theirs. After two days of conducting the most frustrating interviews we had recorded, we were fortunate enough to discover Ngodup Tsering, who our waiter at the Pyramid contacted for us. Namrata had casually asked the waiter if he knew of anywhere we could look for a Tibetan translator as we ate our lunch. Perhaps a nearby school? He disappeared into the recesses of the restaurant and returned five minutes later. "Come and meet him here tomorrow morning at 10:00," he told us.

So now we sit in his house at the Hengja Refugee Camp, the oldest Tibetan refugee camp in Pokhara, cross-legged on a carpet just large enough for the three of us. Our translator himself sits on another, and the shaman sits on the bed, 80 years old and very thin, in the same white T-shirt he wears every day, gray hair on his chin twisted into a thin goatee. The shaman has gained substantial confidence in recent years since he appeared before the Dalai Lama himself, so he no longer heals all people regardless of ability to pay as shamans in Tibet were required to do. He picks cases according to

49

his taste and allows the camp's other shaman to do the rest. According to our translator, this shaman, slight as he looks, possesses a great deal of power; we listen, intrigued, as he relates his story...

When the old shaman was thirteen, he showed signs of power, and his grandfather, an old shaman himself, knew that he was meant to follow in his footsteps. He wanted to open his grandson's nerves and arteries in a special consecration that would allow the gods to enter. So he brought the boy to Mount Kailash to undergo trials in places of spiritual turbulence, the way that countless shamans have ever since Padmasanbhawa came to Tibet seven centuries ago and taught select natives how to control the powers of the gods.

Mount Kailash is said to be home of the Hindu thundergod. Its description seems mythological to me, the mountain of mountains, the one place I am told to go to if I ever make it to Tibet. I imagine it towering to the sky, staggering in its immensity, the white of clouds blending with the white of snow. Around the mountain's base, pilgrims circle in prayer.

The boy, too, had to circle the mountain, performing a *puja* in every sacred place around it. It would take him one year as he did *puja* after *puja* wherever spirits converged as they did in areas where rivers crossed. And at the very end, after 108 *pujas*, the final— possibly fatal—test of Tarka awaited him.

Although his grandfather was there to advise him and many relatives escorted them to the mountain, he had to undergo the tests alone. Those becoming shamans must fend for themselves and resist the overwhelming power of the gods. But he had more guidance than many shamans do because of his grandfather's experience. "Don't lose your concentration," his grandfather told him, offering him a special mirror. He encouraged him and coached him as he performed *puja* after *puja*. The young shaman-in-training swelled with confidence as he succeeded again and again in drawing the gods into himself...

As the boy and his grandfather shaman circled a mountain, they encountered a family. The family members greeted them excitedly, related their troubles: "One year ago, we were camping for the night in this area. But when we woke up in the morning, our daughter-in-law was gone! We searched for her everywhere, but we found no trace of her." They asked the grandfather if he could perform a prophecy to tell them whether she was spirited away by a deity.

The shaman performed the prophetic *puja* asked of him. "The girl is alive!" he announced to their excitement. "She is lying in a cave twenty-five kilometers away from here, half-dead. In the cave where *yetis* and vultures lay eggs—she is still alive, but she is very weak. Go there! You must reach her before midday!"

Seven horsemen raced to the caves. The old shaman instructed six others to assist him as he performed a fire *puja*. A large iron basin elevated above a fire contained white crystal stones. The crystals turned red with heat, and oil was poured upon them. A deity controlling him, the old shaman's body stepped onto the burning stones, chanting, rendering the demi-gods powerless through his ritual.

In the caves, the seven horsemen found the girl, naked and unconscious. By evening, they returned to camp and brought her inside the tent before the grandfather shaman. "Feed her ash-liquid for now," the old man instructed. "She probably has not eaten solid food for a year; she must be nursed back to health slowly..."

The young shaman-in-training was frightened by the lady. She was a sleeping skeleton, skin pulled tight over bones. "Why do we have to stay with her?" he asked his grandfather, hoping for a quick escape now that she had been returned to the people.

The woman did not regain consciousness for days. Her family fed her as the old shaman had instructed, filtering ashes of yak's dung into water with a little bit of syrup. On the fourth day, she opened her eyes. She tried to speak but she could not.

On the sixth day, the woman urinated for the first time.

On the eighth day, her voice finally emerged, feeble from a year of disuse. She spoke of her kidnapping. When she woke up a year ago, she found herself among demi-gods, in a different realm.

"Some people have two spirits—do you believe in that? They have two spirits, that...you know..." our translator attempts to explain.

For it was the girl's spirit that awoke in the presence of the demi-gods and not her physical self, which lay in the cave.

Rabbits were the animals of the demi-gods, and their milk was what she survived on throughout the year. Each day, the demi-gods sent her to pick flowers for them, but they lived in a wintry region, the ground covered with snow. Each day, she would wander desperately, searching for flowers to please them, but return empty-handed to the wrathful deities. They beat her severely for her failure. At times, they sent her to bring them ice from the mountains. By the time she returned with the precious commodity, it had melted to water, and again she was punished.

At times, during her journeys, she felt vaguely aware of her relatives searching for her, but they could not hear her because she was in another realm of existence. Her body remained in the cave where the demi-gods had placed it, and her soul lived with them in their realm. As time went on, her family became a dream, and she felt that she belonged with the demi-gods. When she felt the presence of a relative, she was nearly pulled out of her dream but she never felt strong enough to leave the cave.

When the seven people who rode to her aid removed her from the cave, she had still felt active in the realm of the demi-gods. But then suddenly, an overwhelming flame entered the cave. The demi-gods screamed in terror, running from it. The woman felt faint as it drowned her senses...

Twenty-five kilometers away, the shaman was conducting his fire *puja*, wresting her spirit away from the realm where it had lived for so long.

As he listened to the girl describe her experience, the old shaman deduced who had kidnapped her.

*

"They were not actually demi-gods," our translator explains. "They were local protectors. Each family has a home protector, and local protectors protect villages. Dharma protectors act in different sects of Buddhism, and so on. She was taken by a local protector, not a demi-god."

The girl's family pleaded with the shaman to get rid of the local protector, but he explained to them that he could not do it alone. He instructed a representative from each family of the nearby village to come to their aid, bringing guns and any other weapons they possessed. Once again, the grandfather entered an empowered state and began shooting at the small *stupa* overlooking the village. The villagers joined in his efforts, condemning their local protector, and within minutes, its walls crumbled down. "No more harm will come from this local protector," the old shaman promised.

The village threw together a large party to celebrate the demise of their local protector. Their celebration lasted for a week. The old shaman and his grandson became rich; every house gave them offerings: yaks and horses, meat, curd, butter, cheese…

The boy and his grandfather stayed for two more weeks to treat the malnourished woman. Little by little, she learned to move again, and her bland complexion grew more substantial as she began eating more foods.

An interesting interlude had sidetracked the young shaman's ritual duties, but now, the dangerous places waited…

I am entering that place where skepticism is overcome by potential and my mind is pushed to that in-between area of awed credulity. A girl who was kidnapped by *yetis* from another dimension, who lived on rabbits' milk for a year, her physical body starving slowly in a cave…it seems very real. I feel wonderfully present, my mind awake and alert and racing with possibilities. *This,* I think as he talks, *is what I came for.* And then I push back my thought so I can focus on the story again.

I am reeling with its power as we leave the camp.

We never did reach the end of the shaman's tale. He told us more in another session, of his young days as a shaman, of curing the daughter of a rich family—another tale that he left to be continued. But being the more sought-after shaman, our translator told us that he would expect payment each session for his time. We simply could not afford him.

IX. Memory

Ngodup Tsering remembers how, when he was five years old, he looked over the edge of a plateau and saw a thousand stars fallen from the sky. In reality, these stars were the lights on the helmets of the Chinese army as they swept across the land. Family after family realized the danger and fled. Some heeded warnings of their neighbors while others did not understand what trouble the Chinese could have with them until the army arrived and they ran, clinging to what they could, having to leave fallen family members behind.

When our translator's family arrived in Nepal, officials were standing on the bridge ready to stab them with needles. His father became furiously defensive, thinking they intended to kill them. The Tibetan refugees did not understand that by allowing medical workers to shoot their arms with vaccines, they would become immune to the epidemics plaguing the population. And so early refugees succumbed to widespread disease, dying by the dozen. From the wild area of Tibet, where to this day, nomadic groups live in areas unravished by modern civilization, the refugees entered the kingdom of Nepal, with its foreign culture...

"Every family of refugees has its own story," Ngodup told us.

Remembering our own experience of adapting to Nepal, I think of how much I must leave out. To go continually into the wearying and unsatisfying aspects of my overall experience would be dull as canned vegetables. But so much of the time, that was how it was—wearying, unsatisfying.

Adjusting to Nepal was not easy for Namrata and me. Social interactions were so disconcerting in their Indian-but-not-Indianness that at times, I felt hideously racist for disliking my atmosphere as much as I did. Everyone smiled more than we were used to and stopped smiling more quickly than we were used to when the slightest thing went wrong. The lady selling bananas in a small store on the corner of our street was once kind enough to give us the number we wanted, though we only managed to pull out enough small crumpled bills to pay for half of them. Later, we stopped at the stall and gave her husband the remaining amount. She was apparently not informed of this, however, because every day after that when we passed by, she glared at us angrily, refusing to talk to us, labeling us her enemies with her eyes. This is a mild example, but jumping to rash conclusions seemed the norm wherever we went.

Part of Namrata's and my trouble was that we *looked* like we should be insiders to the culture. People often assumed that we were Nepali. Or that Namrata was Nepali and I was Indian. Neither of us spoke Nepali, though Pabitra's lessons had given us a mild foundation. In a pinch, we could get by with Namrata's Hindi. It still amazes me how many people believed that we were from India if we told them so, even after we spoke to them in English. In Nepal, unlike India, the people we met could not discern that we were from the US as soon as they heard our accents. If we told them we were American, we would confuse them; "But...you look Indian," they would remark, bewildered, usually asking whether one of our parents was white.

Another disorienting aspect was how something that seemed familiar could be so foreign. It was harder for us than starker contrasts would have been; those, we were used to. But in Nepal, we discovered uncanny differences that jolted us from our expectations. Like Hinduism in Nepal, which often contradicted my experiences as well as Namrata's. The idea of sacrificing life for gods struck us as counterintuitive, so we were unnerved when a cab driver pointed to a site where an animal is sacrificed every afternoon. What I saw chained to the Kali temple, soft ears rising delicately with sleep, struck me as alien as I thought of what would become of it. Large English signs and grim officials often barred non-Hindus from temples, another concept we were not used to. "You look Hindu, so they will let you in," a man who was trying to steal our passports told us as we prepared to enter the main shrine at Pashupatinath. He probably assumed that we were Christian since we are American.

In addition to the culture conflict, I am aware of how much our experiences were shaded by the fact that we lived in tourist traps. Although we were not tourists, we were usually treated like tourists, which frustrated us—especially since we could see through facades that most outsiders couldn't. No matter how friendly Lakeside inhabitants and visitors were with one another, we could see the tensions underlying the area. I saw the faces of the locals when foreign tourists pumped naked legs against the pedals of bicycles that would cost an average Nepali a year's worth of wages. I saw the bewilderment of visitors when vendors stalked them in the rain, umbrella against umbrella, refusing to let them pass without buying *something*. Though I sympathized more easily with the locals than the tourists, the uncomfortable dynamic surrounded us constantly, and I am pathetically sensitive to tensions in my environment.

I tried not to allow my experience in the touristy districts to distort my view of the country. A German couple who chatted with Namrata and me when we treated ourselves to our whitewater rafting trip at the end of our travels epitomize the problem with this: "Indians who go abroad want to make something of themselves," they complimented, not foreseeing how ignorant I would consider the remark. They had resented the way that the locals in India had treated them, claiming that they were ever willing to cheat a white person. But Nepal, they told us, is grand; Nepalis treat them well.

X. A Very Interesting Old Man

"Would you like to talk to one of the shamans today, or a very interesting old man?" Ngodup Tsering had asked us on our first visit to the camp.

"Very interesting old man!" I responded promptly although hearing about the lives of older Tibetans was Sara's project, not ours.

He was eighty-six years old and walked slowly but steadily to the room with us, his brown skin crinkling beside brown eyes alive with humor. He seemed to have reached the plateau in old age where the world and all the life in it are simply hilarious. Wispy white hair fell around his face, a moustache and beard, a hat standing tall on his head. He wore rings of turquoise and red coral on nearly all his fingers and carried three prayer wheels.

He called himself the oldest Tibetan souvenir seller in Nepal. When he first came to the country, he caught on that tourists were interested in acquiring Tibetan artifacts. Never mind that he did not speak a word of English; he would use his fingers and toes to communicate the price. If his fingers and toes were all in use and he wished to add another *rupee*, he stuck out his tongue. Our translator demonstrated how this must have looked, and we all laughed.

When the old man spoke, the warmth and humor in his high-pitched voice came through even though we could not understand his words firsthand. He regaled us with his recollections from Tibet. He remembered how *sadhus* from India traveled to Mt. Kailash on pilgrimages, their eyes searing right through him. They refused to eat meat or dairy products. He was amazed and bewildered by their naked feet sinking into the snow as they strode purposefully toward the mountain. He could see that they had special power. He witnessed himself how easily they could calm down angry dogs.

The old man had come to Nepal before the Chinese invasion with his two daughters, then twelve and sixteen. He had been working for the Chinese in 1947-48, transporting things to Mt. Kailash for them. But in 1959, he heard that they were going to invade. The man he was working as a shepherd for decided to leave for India two months before the invasion, leaving him with all the animals. The neighbors told the old man not to worry about the Chinese since he was not rich, but he left anyway, taking his daughters and the animals across Changla Pass into Nepal. In 1960, when his master came back from India to see him, he returned his wealth to him. The old man had nothing else and was going to return to Tibet, but his master shared half the wealth with him, so he went to Tarabot, where he stayed for six years and enjoyed the locals. Our translator's father conducted small trade with him there. He enjoyed himself more than he had in his own country, working as a spinner, mending…grinding buckwheat and making small stones…

In Tibet, he had always been a shepherd, helping his family with their yaks and sheep since he was young. But when he was nearly sixteen, he joined the salt miners several times on their four-month trips to collect salt. Most of the miners were young, but there were one or two older people who knew the ropes. They led and instructed the younger ones.

There were many regulations for the miners in a group to follow to ensure that the salt run went smoothly. Throughout their trip, the miners had to speak in a secret code language to prevent struggles. They could use only good words; for instance, they could not say "knife" to each other directly. If a miner broke a shoe, he had to mend it in a certain way. During the trip, if anyone found something of value, like a needle or long piece of thread or wooden hooks, he had to give it to the head cook without speaking of it to anyone else. All the wealth of a trip had to be shared.

If a miner broke a rule, he would face a specific punishment depending on his misconduct. A miner who said the wrong thing or performed a small offense might have to make milk tea for everyone, and tea was expensive since it came from China. A boy's family would pack him lots of tea on his first mining trip, knowing that he would make mistakes. Otherwise, he could buy it from others in the group.

Committing a larger mistake resulted in a punishment that cost even more money—performing a *puja* for instance. If a miner carried on relations with a woman during the trip, he would not only have to perform an expensive *puja* but also be responsible for any animals that died during the trip. However, he would have to go out of his way to find a girl in the first place. Men and women often led very separate lives in Old Tibet. "A man would have to ride a horse for seven hours and cross many high rivers before he could reach a woman!" the old man told us gleefully. One woman might have six or seven husbands. (When our translator said this, I thought that he might not mean this literally. But in truth, the sons of farmers often did share one wife. If brother farmers each took a wife, they would have to split up the land amongst themselves. By sharing one woman, they could keep the land intact for the next generation.)

He remembered one woman who confronted a salt miner during a trip and accused him of impregnating her. The head of the expedition ordered the man to give all of his yaks to the girl as penance. But the girl was merciful and took only eight sheep.

During a winter trip, the lakes were frozen. Five or six miners would beat the ice all day with a yak's horn and then boil the ice. The salt lake itself looked like an ordinary lake but for a white rock in the middle. The rock, the old man told us, was the protector of the salt lake. Before collecting salt, a group had to send the protector a mixture of yak and cow in butter. Once, a group forgot to send an offering and they could not manage to load the salt onto their goats and sheep. Then the oldest man made a sling of butter and threw it to the rock in the center, and everything went smoothly after that.

When the old man, then a young boy, traveled to trade, he would take along a charm box with medicines for protection, carrying holy herbal pills blessed by a high *lama*, a Tibetan silver coin, and copper. Blessings from Mt. Kailash were especially powerful; precious pills for epidemics could cure both people and animals. If someone had a bad cold, he could take some roots.

Namrata jumped at this opportunity. "Can you tell us about Tibetan medicine that you've taken when you've been sick?" she asked.

The translator's response took us aback: "He says…he has never taken any medicine for an illness."

But…but…eighty-six…but… Having grown up in countries where painkillers and cough drops were administered to us since childhood, we could not believe him. Surely he misunderstood—perhaps he thought that we meant Western medicine rather than Tibetan?

But still he said no, and his alternative astonished us. In Tibet, he explained, a very high-ranking *lama* can chant mantras into clay tablets. Even in Nepal, near Devi's Fall, Tibetans dig different types of clay from the earth, red, white, gray. Mantras are chanted into boiling water, and the clay is mixed in. The clay is made into small balls, and applying a ball of clay to an injury can take away pain; swallowing it can ward off illness. The old man himself has always used blessed clay tablets to cure illness, and he attests to their soundness.

Although the old man is a layman, a Tantric guru trained him in Tibet. He knows special mantras to stop bleeding, both internal and external. If someone has a nosebleed, he has only to chant and it will vanish.

He can do many things with his learning. If a man needs to reach another place very quickly, he can make his speed ten times faster than normal. In 1962, when he needed money, he used his Tantric knowledge to get himself a position as a porter. One man in the camp did not believe in his capabilities and so the others forced the old man to return the twelve *rupees* they had paid him in advance. Angry with the accuser, the old man cast a spell that made the disagreeable man sick.

Once, a woman in the camp was robbed during the night, and she asked him to perform a prophecy to find out who stole the money. However, he did not need to perform a prophecy in that particular case because as he pointed out, the dogs had not barked. So whoever took the money must be someone familiar to them… The others determined quickly that it must have been the man sleeping near her, and the money was returned to the lady…

"You can do prophecies?" I asked, fascinated.

But he was close-lipped about his mystic arts. "That is dangerous information," he told us. He owns many powerful books with delectable secrets that could do harm if they are not carefully manipulated. There was one man in his camp in Tibet, he told us, who possessed many powerful secret books. He could manipulate Black Magic. He fell in love with the wife of another man, and he was desperate for a love charm. One evening, he saw her going out to a field of yaks to relieve herself. Elated, he rushed to the location after she left and collected some of her urine. But the liquid sample actually belonged to a yak. As he cast his spell, the powerful mantra infuriated the yak, which charged at his tent. He was nearly killed.

He made another example of a boy who was traveling to a neighboring village by nightfall. There were long canyon caves along the way. He knew that wolves often lived in these caves, and the thought made him nervous. But he noticed a couple entering the next cave. At midnight, he heard a scream and realized that the man was attacking the woman. He saw a man walk by carrying something on his back. This was the boy's chance to escape. As he rushed past the next cave, he saw the woman's ornaments. He picked them up and ran. Mantras had lured the woman to the canyon

To kill by using witchcraft, the old man told us, the nails or hair or something from the victim must be appropriated. On the western side of Tibet, where the shamans are, witchcraft is frequently employed. On sacrificial days, the people in this region will happily sacrifice a visitor rather than one of their own. In this region, you must never drink tea when you visit someone.

When we asked him if we could take a picture of him, he posed outside in the sun, spinning a prayer wheel in each hand, the third one tucked under his left arm. Each prayer wheel had the prayer "*Om ma né pad mé hoong*" inscribed in it in circles, over and over again. "The jewel in the heart of the lotus" Brad had thought it meant when Namrata and I had come back with the phrase from Swembunath, where a monk told us to repeat it as we circled a *stupa*. But Ngodup explained that there was more to the prayer than that.

The mantra is a universal prayer. Each syllable represents the different realms of sentient beings: *Om*, heaven; *ma*, the demigods; *né*, the earth; *pad*, the animal realm; *mé*, the angry ghost realm; and *hoong*, hell. In each of the realms, beings suffer; there are external sufferings that beings in a realm might have in common, but each individual suffers privately within as well. Suffering, after all, is as relative as anything else in the world. When the old man spins his prayer wheel, speaks the mantra, he prays for all beings in existence, prays to relieve their suffering. Every moment, sentient beings are reborn, into the same realm or into others, born from the womb, from the earth, from eggs—or a final parentless birth in Nirvana, free and without suffering.

XI. Interlude

I am a water junkie. Each day, I drink up several liters—have to. It is a dependency that formed in eighth grade. I carry a water bottle, preferably a big one, everywhere I go.

Tapwater in Nepal was yellow with a particular smell I cannot describe but did not care to shower in. It was worst in the first place we stayed in Thamel, filling toilets like urine. There, I resorted to brushing my teeth with bottled water like most tourists routinely do. I gave that up as soon as we entered Pema Lamo; I hate using good water for anything other than drinking.

During the monsoon, water contamination is especially prevalent, so we had to be careful. Even if it hadn't been monsoon season, we would have taken precautions, refused water that wasn't boiled or filtered in restaurants, eaten only hot food. The added risk of rainy season made us more vigilant.

When I visit India with my family, we spend many hours boiling and cooling water for drinking. In Nepal, Namrata and I bought bottled water. It cost about fifty cents per liter, and I went through far more of it than Namrata. We could tell that despite the seals, many of the bottles had been used and refilled with water. It made no difference whether we bought from a street vendor or grocery store. The heavily crumpled plastic gave it away, especially since so many of the bottles appealed to consumers to crush them after use to ensure that they were not refilled and restocked by store owners. But it didn't hurt us, so we didn't care.

Twice, we managed to lug home a refillable five-gallon *Bisleri* bottle from the "Safeways" store at the intersection. We held it clumsily, shifting it back and forth between us. Brad and Sara, who

SHILPA KAMAT

had recommended it, had an easier time; their hotel was across the street from the store. Brad used it as a weight, did repetitions in their room.

I read in the newspaper several weeks into our trip that bottled water was 10 to 30% contaminated, *Bisleri* being the safest brand. The only foolproof water is boiled or filtered, but we did not have a stove or access to a filter. We decided to buy *Bisleri* if we could, and if the restocked bottles were filled with common filtered water, it was better for us anyway.

There is nothing more pressing than the mundane necessity of good water.

XII. The Elders

During the rainy season, there is a Tibetan saying that roughly translates to: "May I become sick during this time—but that I may be alive at the end." An old woman at Prithvi Cowk, a Tibetan refugee camp in Katmandu, explained the dangers of working through the monsoon without good rain gear, carrying animal skins that absorb the rain.

We asked her about the main difference she feels between life in Nepal as compared to Tibet. She replied that she suffered a lot during the revolt in Tibet. She lost her parents, her family.

But she misses the food. "It is not available here," she told us, "even if you have money."

As we listened to the stories of the older refugees, I kept vaguely in mind the fact that the Tibetan elders have turned to traditional medicine all their lives. But frankly, I was happy we were sharing a translator with Sara, glad to have an excuse to hear more about the lives of the people we spoke to in addition to their experiences with medicine. In a way, I was becoming more interested by her project than our own.

Most of the lives of older refugees were touched deeply with suffering during the Chinese invasion. As one woman recounted her experience for us, she cried for the children she lost as they fled. We talked to two Campa fighters, veterans of the failed coup, who spoke of their experience in battle. One showed us his knee, where he suffered a bullet wound.

Before the occupation, most of them had lived simple, stable lives. The first old lady we interviewed told us that she feels life in Tibet is physically harder but mentally more peaceful than life in Nepal.

Tibetan nature, she and others agreed, is very friendly; people never quarrel over small things. Most of the elders we interviewed were nomads, living simply as they traveled about the land.

Mo Punjhaam, a seventy-eight-year-old woman, explained the details of life in old Tibet to us. When babies are born, she told us, they are fed with breastmilk for the first few months. After that, they are fed "*paksé*": butter, sugar, and salt are mixed in a special pot for children, stirred and stirred into a thin porridge.

When nomadic children are old enough, they look after the animals—there is no choice in the matter. Seventy-seven-year-old Mutub Lamo recalled how she collected yak dung to use as fuel for fire. She laughed, telling us that when children first begin to lose their teeth, they should be put to work with the yaks; when they are about nine or ten and have a full set of teeth again, they move on to taking care of the sheep. They sleep outside with the animals to protect them from predators. Once, she was attacked by a wolf but did not know it, she told us, laughing again. She thought that it was a big dog.

All the old ladies spoke of the women's labor, what a girl begins to do when she is older. They would milk the animals early in the morning from 3:30 to 6:30 and again in the afternoons from 1:00 to 3:00. First the goats and sheep were milked, then the yaks. It was up to the women to make all the milk products, to transform it into yogurt or butter or cheese. They would start boiling the milk, taking care not to let it go sour. Mutub Lamo explained that yogurt could be made in four hours' time by boiling the milk and then letting it cool to room temperature, mixing some of the yogurt from the last batch in as a culture. Hearing her describe this reminded me of how much I love homemade yogurt, which I eat whenever I am visiting India. It doesn't set very well in the States since the climates in places I've lived are usually cooler, and atmosphere makes a difference in taste. Or maybe it is the quality of the milk.

If you want to make cheese, she continued, you can put in even more yogurt in the boiled milk and let it sit covered until it is very hard. She would shake this curd in a drum made of an animal's skin or belly until she could see butter floating on the surface. She would collect the butter into a different pot, then drain the liquid from the yogurt. The yogurt was then pressed into cheese and stored to dry.

Nomads could pay their taxes with a portion of these milk products.

When a woman is eighteen, her parents arrange her marriage as quickly as possible. Nineteen is a bad age, Mo Punjhaam said. Everyone believes it is bad luck to marry a nineteen-year-old: "Even if she has a crown worth ten times your worldly property, don't marry her." Perhaps it is an unlucky astrological number. Nineteen is not *too old* to marry—marrying after nineteen is all right. She told us that she herself got married at the age of twenty.

Every two or three months, there is a black month during which new things should not be started. A girl and boy can become engaged, but should postpone their marriage until a better time. Mo Punjhaam vividly recalls all the marriage customs. If the child of a rich family is getting married, she said, the woman's family gives an animal if they are nomadic, cash if they are farmers. Dowry is divided into four sections. First, the girl's family divides their ornaments for each of their daughters. Next, the animals are divided amongst the family members. If there are 100 sheep and ten family members, then each person gets ten. Third, monetary assets such as silver boxes are divided, and lastly, clothes that have been in the family for generations. A boy from a rich family would expect all of these things from the family of his bride. He himself would give her parents animals as an offering—a yak or a nice horse, perhaps. They might give gold earrings weighing more than 25 grams with turquoise or coral embedded within.

It is easier to be a servant than rich, Mo Punjhaam told us. Because if you are rich, you have to take care of your servants and their families as well.

"Were you rich?" we asked her.

She was not very rich, she replied, but she did not have to beg. She declared that she now survives in Nepal by the grace of the Dalai Lama.

For most of the women we interviewed, their weddings were memorable times that stood out from the otherwise routine way of life in Tibet. But Chuntume, 69, had a different story when she spoke of marrying at twenty-five. "Can you tell us about your wedding?"

we asked her as she smiled at us, tall and thin, her hair shorn close to her head.

"I never had a wedding," she said. She explained that the servant of a chieftain had been staying with her family. While he was staying with them, she fell in love with him and he with her. So he never left. They had no children, but it did not matter to them. They were happy together for forty-one years, she told us, tears in her eyes; her husband died of diarrhea a few years ago.

As we spoke to the elders, I committed their faces and words to memory to what extent I could, but it was not always easy. For one thing, the stories of many older Tibetans we spoke to before coming to Hengja Camp were badly translated. There was the monk we spoke to who told us how he joined the monastery as a child because he had past life memories of being a monk. We were intensely curious about hearing his memories, but our translator at the time was not much help, and the interview tape ended before he revealed the most interesting parts of what he had to say. We could not have his words re-translated later as we did with some of our other tapes.

Sometimes my wandering attention did not do justice to the people we talked to, especially when I was unwell. One old man had a fascinating tale that he told us in two days about being a translator for the Dalai Lama during negotiations in India. Even as I recorded what he said, I could not impress the interview upon my slumping mind, could not pay close attention to his features or the nuances of his voice when he spoke. I was frustrated with myself, though technically, it did not matter since his story was not a part of my project. As for my project, I knew somewhere in the back of my mind that Namrata and I had to broaden its dimensions somehow, or I would not make it through the last few weeks.

XIII. Sun

The dizzying heat of summer days in Nepal may not be all that different from India, but in India, I had spent more time indoors, under fans. Walking in the sun exhausted us. It was especially bad in the middle of the day, sunlight full and hard as a false smile. At night, the atmosphere simmered down to a tolerable temperature, but the broiling days were traumatizing.

So when I heard that initially, Tibetan refugees did not shed their multiple layers of cloth and fur after entering Nepal's more temperate climate, I could not imagine how they could bear the heat. Their actions made sense, of course; although summers in Tibet were milder compared to the frigid winters, shedding layers of clothing during the summer was considered a bad idea. As Ngodup explained, while the sun may be hot one minute, the next, it may disappear entirely, leaving you shivering. So, reluctant to shed their garments and risk disease, they suffered heatstroke.

I was quite happy to wear my cotton *salwars* and short-sleeved shirts. I did not let myself regret that I could not wear shorts; I am too old to show off my legs in that part of the world—partly to be socially acceptable, partly to prevent the nuisance of twenty men following me down a street. In any case, I loved my *salwars*. They were fit for anything—slightly dressy if we were going to a restaurant or to visit someone, but flexible enough to hike in or climb trees in. They were the most comfortable clothes I owned.

I was wearing one of my cotton *salwars* on the day Namrata and I finally made it to the path leading to the *stupa* we had failed to reach twice. The cab driver let us out at the bottom of the hill on the opposite side of the lake, pointing out that he could not drive us to the top; the road was too rough for a car. So we walked up, and I found the climb enjoyable but knew that Namrata may not be able to go too far with her ankle still bandaged. When we were about halfway up, we stopped, wondering if we would ever make it to the *stupa*. I propped Namrata's ankle on a rock, and our conversation drifted to the rut we were in with our research. It was doing us no good, I pointed out, to keep asking questions about the technicalities of practicing Tibetan medicine. We would only hear the same answers, and there are already many books written about it, anyway. Namrata agreed that we needed to put a new spin on our focus. As we thought about it, she suggested a motivational boost: if we managed to complete a set number of interviews, she said, we should reward ourselves by doing something wild—parachuting, or whitewater rafting, maybe. I agreed.

And then I had an epiphany. I thought of how Tibetan medicine is inextricably linked with Tibetan Buddhism. How despite the science of it, faith plays an integral role in diagnosing, in healing. This was what made the family of Doctor Labsang Lama's patient go to him before considering any other doctor. Why Ani Karin needed to feel a karmic connection with a doctor to trust that he or she could cure her. I thought of how what we were learning from the people we interviewed was the personal aspect of healing—the part of Tibetan medicine that cannot be quantified and recorded.

This wasn't *such* an original epiphany. It was, in a way, what I had wanted to do all along. But it refreshed me to acknowledge to myself how religion and worldview linked with our research as much as the more technical aspects of healing.

As we walked down the hill, we drew the attention of two teenaged boys who tried to flirt with us. Seeing Namrata's ankle, they asked if we needed help. "He is a doctor," one said, pointing to the other. We shook our heads and moved on. They followed at a polite distance, serenading us with bits of Hindi songs. "Maybe they don't understand," one whispered to the other in Nepali, and so the boy sang a line in English: "Everything I do—I do it for you!"

Thoroughly amused, Namrata and I waved at them as we crossed the street at the bottom of the hill to take a cab home.

XIV. Illness

Like Tibetan Buddhism, Tibetan medicine sees the body as formed from cosmic elements that must remain in balance for good health. But human beings often tend to go to extremes, forgetting balance, and each person has three ways of inviting disease: through *dochak*, attachment, especially attachment to sex; through *shetang*, anger; or through *timuk*, ignorance. The mind controls all of these, explained Tibetan doctor Gyurmey Dorjee. He was wise and knowledgeable, and we were fortunate to learn from him. The oldest doctor in Pokhara, he has been practicing medicine for fifty-five years since he was fifteen. He taught us the basics, explaining how the five cosmophysical elements—earth, water, fire, air, and space—create microorganisms, and an imbalance of the elements causes disease.

If your attachments are too strong, they may cause *loong*, an imbalance of air that makes you feel weak. *Loong* is the easiest to diagnose; you can see it in a person's complexion, in the pulse and the eyes. The air enters your vein when your energy drops, and you may feel a suddenness, an abnormality. If it travels to the heart, you will feel a physical disturbance; if it travels to the brain, you will feel mentally disturbed. Air represents thinking, and if a person's *loong* is balanced, then she is peaceful, happy, sharp…if not, she is lazy and hot-tempered…

If you are too angry, your fury may cause *tippa*, an imbalance of bile. This may cause a fever. The bile may be inflamed, or liquid may have increased in the bile, or the liquid in the bile may be inflamed. This seemed a bit confusing, and he said more about this that was lost in translation, but I remember that Dr. Choekyi told me that my stomach problem was caused by a bile imbalance—I am not sure what this means. Jaundice is a more concrete example of a disease caused by a bile imbalance. So is Hepatitis B. Fire is the cosmophysical element related to *tippa*.

Ignorance, an excess dullness, can cause *begane*, hurting the digestive system. This is also caused by eating food that throws off the body's balance. *Begane* is an earth and water imbalance. The earth is stable, water light, so *begane* can have a variety of symptoms. In any case, this is apparently what Namrata and I had, *begane*, caused by the ignorance of what was in our food at the restaurant we went to with Sara. I remember staring in annoyance at a blown-up picture of Britney Spears as the three of us waited for our food. We should have been clued off by the fact that no one else was in the restaurant.

During the worst monsoon rains that Pokhara had seen in years, Namrata and I lay shivering under blankets at the Lake Palace. As thundering water washed away houses from hills, I dashed madly to the bathroom again and again, unable to hold any food in my stomach.

It was just before the rain started in the afternoon when we fell ill all at once, realizing our fevers at Once Upon A Time as a Nepali guy studying in New Zealand prattled about bamboo groves. ("Are you from New Zealand?" he had started the conversation, thinking us Maori.) For some unknown reason, we had dragged ourselves from our beds, where we had collapsed after coming back from interviewing, to go to the restaurant. The sun stared us down with merciless heat as we walked to the main street, and I closed my eyes, blind to the cow dung splotching the ground. At the restaurant, we slurped up our *lassis* but were unable to take more than two bites from the plates of cheeseless lasagna we had ordered. Namrata was silent on her chair, and I smiled stupidly at the forestry student's grand plan of making millions by planting bamboo groves while adding green to the earth. We were trying not to collapse. "Do you want to go to a club tonight?" Mr. New Zealand asked.

After yielding to temptation and checking my e-mail next door, I raced back, feeling faint, only to find the bathroom occupied by Namrata. I had the room key in my pocket, and she lamented that she had exploded at Deepak for teasing her by pretending he had no spare key.

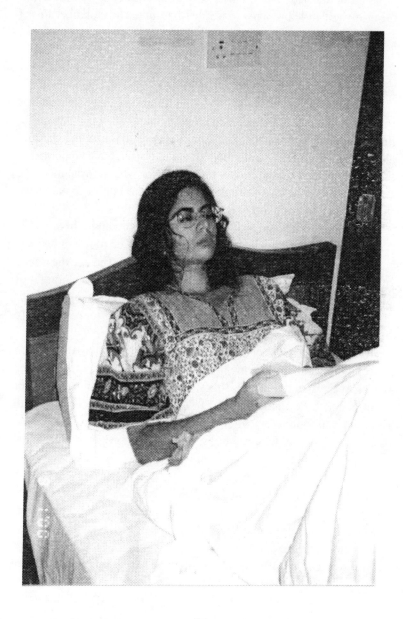

Bamboo man's name and hotel address were on a yellow napkin in the pocket of my jeans, which lay discarded on the floor as I huddled under bedcovers. I was shivering with cold but could not bring myself to leave what warmth I had under my blanket to get another one. I was overjoyed when Sara and Brad paid us a visit. They brought me a second blanket, poured water from the five-liter *Bisleri* bottle sitting next to my bed into a cup. They even offered to stay overnight in case we needed anything.

Namrata and I had avoided ordering room service because it was ingrained in us to consider it a waste of money even if it wasn't all that expensive in Lake Palace. Now, I was so thankful that I could slip my arms out from under bedcovers and stretch to the phone on the bedside stand to dial up the restaurant for what nourishment we needed. In the next day, I drank more soda than I do in a year as we nibbled sparsely on plain toast and boiled potatoes.

I developed a fear of food. The complex carbohydrates of *tandoori paneer* that tempted me threatened to wreak havoc to my intestines. Less insidious foods I could not palate; when placed beside the image of golden-brown tofu slices and steaming vegetables, the thought of plain toast was too one-dimensional for my taste buds to bear.

Slowly, I shrank. My already oversized jeans became uncomfortably loose.

My decline scared Namrata. She was used to my eating much more, having to wait for me at restaurants as I finished my meals, which were usually twice the size of her own. She no longer complained how Indians spend too much time preoccupied with finding good food to eat when they travel. She now encouraged me to eat. But I did not trust my body, and without proper nutrition, the elements took their time regaining their balance inside me.

There is more to Tibetan medicine than a literal belief in the elements—the talk of elements often represents the more technical terms that Western science might use to talk of a disease. The doctors, who understand the subtleties of the elements and how they balance each other, can read from the pulses what an allopathic physician would have to ask a long series of questions to determine, have been able to diagnose in the same way for thousands of years. Every herb used in Tibetan medicine is the same as it was 2,000 years ago—the same name, the same plant, the same way of healing.

The different herbs represent each of the five cosmophysical elements. Because the herbs have grown up in balance, they cure imbalance the same way the existence of the needed elements would. Each and every grain is related to afflictions of the elements.

Even cancers may be cured by Tibetan medicine if they are detected early. If a tumor has grown for more than a few weeks, it is very difficult. At Hengja Camp, our translator introduced us to Norbu Gyaltsen, a forty-eight-year-old man who showed us his knee; one year before, it had been swollen with cancer. Western doctors tested the tumor. They took an X-Ray and sent it to England. When the results came back, they told him they would have to operate, and the man refused to have surgery. He decided he would just die, he told us.

But Doctor Kaycha, a traditional Tibetan physician, treated him effectively. First, he covered the knee with a bandage of herbs. After five days, he took the bandage off and re-wrapped the knee. Now, the cancer under control, the bone of the knee still protrudes excessively. If Norbu Gyaltsen had been treated earlier, then there would have been no permanent damage. He hopes that maybe the bone will straighten out in time. He is very grateful that he did not have to operate and continues taking the medication. It is expensive, one tablet costing sixteen *rupees*. But they are worth it; Tibetan herbs that are painkillers last longer than Western medicines. Remembering how his knee used to be shakes him. Though the medicine has worked well so far, he fears a relapse.

Doctor Dorjee told us he would be attending a conference on cancer in Dharamasala, showed us a pamphlet of the agenda the doctors there would discuss. They are working on a way to treat AIDS.

When Namrata and I were well enough to get out of bed, we

decided to go to a doctor to make sure we had not swallowed parasites. We were not so feverish anymore, but my stomach was still queasy and unable to hold much food. After a sluggish day of interviewing, my mind on the plain digestive biscuits I had bought instead of the speaker, we asked a cab driver to take us to the allopathic doctor our translator had recommended.

We waited on the pavement outside the clinic for our names to be called, pulling as far away from the crowd of other patients as we could. It started to rain, which no one was too happy about. I stared blandly at the uneven stones cemented under our feet, at the other patients. A woman clutched a coughing baby. Namrata and I glanced at one another wearily. We wondered why we had bothered to come, whether we might catch something worse from the other patients as we waited.

Finally, the woman at the window called us up. I filled out a form, and we went in to the smiling doctor. An unknown man followed us about the clinic, standing in the background even during the examination.

The doctor treated us kindly. "Are you really from India?" he asked, disbelieving. He did not appear too concerned about our illness as he asked about our symptoms. "Did you eat meat there?" he asked when I conjectured that the food had made us ill. He beamed at us when he learned we were vegetarian. "Great! Vegetarians are the healthiest people. They live the longest lives." He told us we had nothing to worry about.

I was reassured that we did not show symptoms of any horrible diseases, but I was mainly concerned with having a stool test performed. For some reason, the receptionist thought this hysterical. When we went back to check the results, the sheet the lab handed me showed that I did not have a parasite, and so Namrata decided her body was also safe. I walked back to hand the sheet to the doctor, as the lab people instructed. He looked at the results and translated the chart for me, confirming what I had already deciphered. He gave me a scrawled prescription for flu-like symptoms, and I stuffed it in my pocket, thanking him, knowing I would never use it; I did not want to take the medicine. Did not want to ingest strong things with unpredictable side effects—superfluous drugs. He did not say the pills were necessary. I was getting better on my own.

I wondered about my reaction to it all, my in-between state of mind. On one hand, I did want evidence, evidence that only an allopathic clinic could provide: a scientific test to make sure there was nothing in me that was keeping me sick. On the other, I did not like the way their medicine would work on me if I took it, playing with my immune system as it tried to purge me of whatever it was that I had. I liked the straight-forwardness of the Tibetan method, the way its physicians had the ability to tell *me* what I had rather than my having to essentially diagnose myself—but at the same time, when something happened, I still ran to an allopathic doctor.

In retrospect, it doesn't make sense. There were so many practicing traditionalists in the vicinity, their offices stocked with herbal cures. I could have gone to them instead, gone to them as well. Part of it was that my parents wanted me to see an allopathic physician, cajoled me over the phone to have testing done, just to be sure. Perhaps the frantic appeals of my mother, who does not trust any medicines she does not *know*, prevented me from taking a chance on herbal remedies. But really, I think, it's like a religion. Even the doubting run back to what they know in times of need.

Some diseases cannot be cured with herbs. Past lives, Doctor Dorjee explained, can affect present health. Actions during a past life or things that may have happened to the soul in another lifetime may affect a patient. We know if there is *karma* at work, the doctor explained, if the usual methods fail to cure. These pains, such as a feeling of inadequacy, take a long time to cure, require selflessness, detachment, and renunciation. Bad spirits from interactions in previous lives can also harm us in the present, returning to demand compensation. Ulcers may be caused by past life influences. Patients may need to make pilgrimages to counteract the influences. Stomach ulcers are curable, but ulcers between the esophagus and the stomach or cancer of the stomach are not. Doctors are trained to distinguish whether a disease is caused by physical elements, baggage from past lives, or bad spirits.

There are medicines for madness as well. A person suffering from a mental disorder can take herbs, take medicine that has been blessed by the Dalai Lama, or wear blessed amulets that counteract the brain illness. And there are other ways... As skeptical as readers might be about some of these methods, Tibetan healing excels in treating mental illness beside its allopathic counterpart. Because, I think, Tibetan healing acknowledges the crucial role of the mind in inflaming and curing illness.

XV. Story

During the height of our interviewing, one of the best things I did was take two more days off to humor my lingering illness. I enjoyed the time alone, curling up in bed absorbed in my book—*Midnight's Children* by Salman Rushdie, a book I had started several times only to stop on the third page. I left the hotel room only at lunchtime, wanting toast and soda somewhere other than my hotel for once. The Pyramid makes its own bread and the lemon is served fresh with plain carbonated water, a gourmet meal compared to my usual squares of white toast and sugary 7-Up. After eating, I climbed to the Internet café above the restaurant and e-mailed to my heart's content, ignoring the seven-*rupee*-a-minute charge. Simply avoiding the diesel-guzzling trucks that filled our lungs as we rode to and from the refugee camp made me feel better.

So did reading. In fact, I feel like *Midnight's Children* got me through Nepal. When I had arrived in the country after three months abroad, I had needed a break rather than a research project. The air pollution in Bombay had already worked up my allergies, and the air in Nepali cities was no better. It shook me how disconnected I felt from everything around me.

So much of the time, I felt nothing. I would march rotely through searing sunlight, stare blankly into the greens surrounding the lake, puzzled by why they were not moving me. I would smile mechanically at the two-year-old across from our hotel as she called *"Namaste!"* to every person passing by her parents' store—everyone else who passed the store thought she was cute. Their faces opened up with a universal "how cute" expression. It scared me that even children aroused no emotions in me. *I love children*, I told myself, but felt nothing. When I talked to Sara and Brad, I turned stupid—inarticulate, oblivious, overflowing with redundant questions.

The future was consuming my mind, which throbbed with thoughts of being home in Georgia, starting college again, feeling winter term with friends and the wonderful Minnesota chill. I was driving Namrata crazy; she is used to my entrenching myself in the now and growing wildly excited by every footprint and crooked tree that catches my eye. As we passed through Nepal, I could not stop talking of everything I had left hanging in the States, of everything I wished to go back to.

And then the sickness hit, making me even more homesick.

But as I read, I stopped. The life of the narrator, filled with everyone he knew, sidled into me. Paragraphs did the job that flat pink Pepto Bismal tablets could not. From pickles to telepathic conferences to old television commercials I had never seen, they brought everything inside me to life, appealing to all my senses and stuffing my mind with speculations. They pushed me deep into the moment, prodded my hand back to a pen. They made me emote again.

Story can be a powerful medicine.

But magic realism is a contemporary concept. A new twist on an old tradition, mixed with satire and contemporary cleverness. Before, when the fantastic was treated as real, it was just a tale. It performed the same function of taking listeners outside themselves, injecting them into someone else, making them think about life, making them wonder.

The oldest souvenir seller in Nepal wanted us to buy souvenirs from him. In exchange for his time, it was the least we could do; we went to his house with him and looked through his trinkets and his daughter's jewelry, each of us selecting carefully. I bought a pair of dice, a Tibetan coin, and a lapis bracelet.

Delighted, he told us that he would talk to us now whenever we wanted. Today, he said, he would tell us a story his grandparents told him. We listened as Ngodup translated the four-hour tale:

Once upon a time (I will interject because this is an old tale, and since I'm translating to English, I may as well invoke Western tradition) there lived a family with three sons in the western region of Tibet. The three sons were nearing manhood as sons generally do sooner or later.

By and by, the father asked his oldest what he wished to pursue in life, and the son dutifully replied that he wished to be a tailor. With his father's approval, he dedicated his life to sheering cloth and measuring waist sizes, stitching a fine seam around financial stability.

Then the father went to the second son, asking him what he wished to make of his life. "I'll be a carpenter!" the boy declared, and proceeded to slice through wood with a passion, building sturdy things into which he carved fine patterns. If you measure success by money, then he was what you would call successful in his endeavors.

Now, the third son evoked great hopes in his father, for he was very clever and handsome, and the father foresaw a promising future of reaping vicarious pleasure from his son's achievements. But when he asked his son what he wished to pursue, the boy answered with the nonchalant air of a born slacker, "Oh, I don't really know."

As I put this tale into words, I think of the namelessness of heros. They are kept vague, their qualities never specific. It is difficult to write about at times, the boy did this, the boy did that. My mind craves detail. But to name him would be too much of a liberty; I am already imposing too many labels on this story.

"Be decisive!" the father told him. "You must be *something!*"

"Oh, I suppose I could just stay near the house and look after the sheep and horses," the boy said, "I enjoy that." As all Tibetan children, he had begun tending yaks at the age of seven, and then horses and sheep.

Such infantile work would not satisfy the father. "You're a man now! You must pursue some trade!"

So at length, the boy promised him that he would think of

something, and in the meantime, he took care of sheep and horses. He grew fascinated with the idea of making bridles for horses. *Perhaps I can do this professionally*, he mused. He put his whole-hearted efforts into his craft...but the bridle, though elegant and fashionable, was too small to possibly fit any of the horses. (For all his intelligence, the youngest son never had been good with proportions.)

But on the night of the first Tibetan month's full moon, a horse had a baby, and the bridle fit the foal perfectly. The boy admired the way his handiwork fit onto the sleek foal, knowing that the horse complemented the bridle rather than the other way around.

And then he was taken by surprise as the foal spoke to him. "I must warn you," he said. "The ogre who lives in the East caught your father today! Don't ask how, I just know. Anyway, your father has convinced the ogre to let him free in exchange for *you*! This very evening, he will come for you. Your whole family will undoubtedly cry and ask what you want to take with you. When that happens, tell your family that you want me, your horse who wears the first bridle you ever made. Please trust me, and I won't let you down!"

The son was now in quite a predicament. He remembered the ogre who was rumored to reside in the eastern region where bushes that were commonly used for fire fuel grew with no thorns. In his family's region, these bushes, small and yellow-flowered, were well endowed with sharp needles to protect themselves. As he thought about it, he realized that his father may have ignored the border dividing east and west to gather the enticing bushes on the other side. So although a special *puja* had been performed, promising the ogre that no one of their region would take the thornless bushes if he gave them no trouble, the ogre now had reason for revenge...

When the boy returned to his home, he found his family distraught. Mournfully, his father told him how he had taken two bushes from the eastern region for which the ogre demanded repayment; the boy was to go. His family, as the horse predicted, lamented the boy's departure and asked him what he wished to take with him. *Well, the foal was right so far*, he figured, and asked as instructed only for the new foal and bridle.

His family willingly gave him the foal and bridle as well as a small blanket and a saddle that was too big for the small horse. The son thanked them and went on his way. The events at hand apparently did not phase him too much. He always did have more faith in horses than people...

There I go again, imposing thought. That is the way I can be, I sometimes impose thought on myself, picked up the habit from people in my environment as I was growing up. So I can't help from imposing thought as I write characters I must think for. But it works, doesn't it?

On their way to the neighboring region, crossing the border took a long time. As they reached the other side, the foal startled the boy by lying on the ground and rolling over and over. As he rolled, he grew larger and larger so that when he got up, he was full-grown. There he stood before the boy, bright white and glowing with energy and strength. The bridle had grown with the horse, and the blanket and saddle now fit comfortably on his back. "Jump on," he told the boy.

"Oh, you didn't have to bring a horse!" the ogre exclaimed, content upon his arrival. "I have plenty. In any case, I'm hoping that you'll be of use as a protector! So...now for a little test. I want to know how powerful you are. So either I'll go up to the roof and you try to shoot me from below or you go and I'll try to shoot you."

"Oh, I suppose you can try and shoot me," the boy told him. Happy at the confidence the boy felt in his safety, the ogre sent his most powerful arrow shooting up to the boy, who waited on the roof. The arrow, however, only reached halfway before falling.

So the ogre exchanged places, and the boy grasped his bow tightly. Going to the temple, he took aim. The arrow shot straight at the ogre on the roof and killed him instantly.

"Hmm," mused the boy. "I guess I'm free of the ogre now. I don't really have anything else to do…"

So he decided to keep wandering east. Mounting his horse, he galloped farther into unknown territory. A day passed uneventfully, but by late afternoon on the second day, the boy and horse came across a man who lay on the ground, staring above him.

"Hello," he said as he approached. "What are you doing?"

"I," the man declared with importance, "am a great hunter. I am *hunting*. As you can see, there are ghouls flying above us. I am waiting, for I have shot one, and it is taking its time to die. Ghouls are funny that way."

The boy waited with the man as the ghouls spiraled eerily above him. Eventually, one of them fell to the ground, an arrow in its chest, and he looked on admiringly. "If you're homeless," the boy said, "then why don't we travel together? I don't have a home either; I was offered to an ogre, but now he's dead."

"I don't have a horse, though," the man mused. "I wouldn't be able to keep up!"

"Oh, just touch my horse's tail, and say this prayer…" the boy instructed, chanting a line.

The man did as instructed, and upon speaking the words, a second horse of the same kind stood before him. He climbed on accommodatingly, and the two men and horses journeyed on. As they passed through a very plain valley, they saw another man who leaned oddly between two hills.

"Hello," they greeted him. "Who are you?"

"I'm the strongest man in the region," he announced, flexing his ample muscles. "I lift these hills for a good workout—I've just lifted them ten times."

"Can you show us?" the boy asked, and the man heaved the hills higher into the sky with a grunt, supporting their weight for a moment before placing them back onto the earth. Impressed by his strength, the boy and the hunter asked the hill-lifter to join them.

"But I have no horse…" he objected. Quick to act, the boy took a strand of his horse's tail and set it on fire.

"Hold this," he said, giving Hill-lifter the burning strand, "and repeat this prayer after me…"

Three men rode three identical horses deeper into the east. As they journeyed, they came across a large lake. Making their way around the shores, they found a man sitting in a meditative posture with his feet on his thighs. Greeting him pleasantly, they asked what he was up to.

"I am Lake-drinker," he told them staunchly. "I can take in this entire lake in one sip—watch," he commanded, touching his mouth to the water. And with one large slurp, the lake was drained of water, a stray fish flopping about for a moment before he spewed the water back out. "I'm not too thirsty just now," he explained.

"Impressive!" the boy exclaimed. "The three of us are on a journey to the realm of the eastern goddess. We would be honored if you would accompany us."

"Sounds like a good adventure," the man told them, "but I have no horse…"

Repetitions lukewarm and slippery. Easier in a tale than if they were real. But transcription is hard on me, plodding, forcing me to write in straight lines, the beginning to the end. I like writing stories all at once, like meditations.

Four men on horses rode into the realm of the eastern goddess. One possessed great skill as a hunter. One could lift hills as easily as a twig. One could outdrink an army of men, destroying ecosystems of lakes wherever he went. And one could make fantastic bridles for horses.

The boy's horse, the powerful original, slowed down. "What's wrong?" the boy asked, and listened closely to the response.

"Come and collect me tomorrow before the others are awake," the horse told him. Each night, when the men set up camp to sleep, the horses stayed slightly farther away. In the morning, one of the men would bring them back to camp, then the four would ride off. But the next morning, the boy came dutifully to his horse's side before the others were awake. "We are already in the realm of the

Eastern Goddess," the horse told him. "If you want her, come with me—I will send the other horses to your friends, don't worry about them."

"Okay," said the boy, hopping onto his horse obediently.

After some time, the boy and horse arrived at a hill shaped like a heart. There was no path across it, but the horse stopped and began digging. As the horse pulled away a big rock, a path to the top of the hill suddenly revealed itself before the boy's astonished eyes.

Up they climbed, and the boy felt that they were nearing the top of the sky. When they were nearly at the entrance of the goddess's abode, the horse spoke once again. "Listen to me carefully. There are tigers guarding the castle. They do not permit any living thing to enter alive—but just take a piece of my tail, and when we enter this realm, stay behind me. I know how to defeat them. Leave me to the tigers, but don't cry—I will kill them, and they will kill me, but don't cry—when you need me, I will return to you."

True to his word, the horse leaped at the tigers upon entering the abode. Distraught, the boy watched as his horse sacrificed itself to the tigers. But he remembered what the horse had told him and did not burst into tears. Hanging on to the piece of the horse's tail, he pushed his way farther into the home of the goddess.

And he entered the room, he saw her, standing alone, surrounded by invisible demi-gods who served her faithfully. Mad with grief or filled with self-importance, it is up to you to decide which, he declared, "Accept me as a husband, for I have overcome many obstacles to get you—or I'll chop you into pieces!"

Strangely attracted to the boy's domineering presence, the goddess accepted him. They fell into quite a happy marriage, but the boy was not entirely content with his conquest because he could not succeed in calling back his dead horse. Each day, he left the mountaintop to search for him as well as for his friends, clutching the forlorn strand of tailhair, but he would return in the evening unsuccessful. (His sense of direction must have matched his sense of proportion.)

My attention, name it American or modern, can wander, but I

*don't know if it is the result of fast-paced television or any of that. I
do not think in linears, am often lost when people must talk from one
thing leading directly to the next with no jumps.*

*The old man, telling the tale, enthused all the way through. Myself,
enthused but needing space to think, and space is something that
gets lost in translation.*

*Or maybe it is the process of translation that gives the mind room
to wander as we wait for each segment of the story. No breaks when
we need breaks, and breaks when we don't. It has been more than
two hours.*

Ever since the horse had revealed the path to the goddess's
mountaintop realm, people for miles around could see it. In the west,
a powerful kingdom existed, and the king of the region wanted his
son to wed the goddess. "Whoever can bring that goddess here to
wed my son may have half my possessions," he declared generously.

Thrilled by the prospect, an old lady volunteered herself. "I'll do
it!" she declared, and the king encouraged her warmly.

Perhaps a normal old lady would not have had the stamina to
climb to the top of a mountain on her own from a different region,
but this old lady was in actuality an ogress. In no time, she was at the
entrance to the realm, and she appealed forlornly to the goddess:
"I'm an old lady who has no one to look after me, so please let me
stay here forever—if not forever, then at least a year—if not even
this, then at least a month, please, for I'm old and weak!"

When her husband returned home, the goddess related the
woman's request to him, and he shrugged good-naturedly. "Sure,
why not? We have loads of room!"

The next day, when her husband left, the cunning ogress
confronted the goddess. "Your husband—I see he's a very powerful
man," she commented casually. "I don't suppose he's told you where
his power lies?"

The goddess, naïve from having spent all the years of her life
sheltered on a mountaintop, fingered the necklace that her husband
had presented to her. "He told me it lies in this necklace," she declared.

A wrinkled hand grasped the necklace, ripping it apart. Beads scattered, and the goddess despaired, but that evening, her husband returned as usual. The goddess said nothing to him of the incident, believing his powers to be truly great.

Of everyone in the story, I think the hardest for me to relate to is the goddess.

The ogress, irritated by her failure, approached the goddess again. "Obviously, your husband doesn't trust you," she told her. "Why else did he lie to you about where his power lies?"

"Oh, don't say that," the goddess objected. "He's such a good man, and we love each other very much. We've been living here so happily—why would he lie to me?"

But the ogress's insinuations worked upon her mind, so she admitted that night when they were alone how the necklace was broken. "Why did you lie to me?" she cried, and her husband, perplexed by her angst, admitted that his true power lay not in the necklace but in his knife.

From the next room, two ogress-ears that hear what a normal old lady would never be able to hear registered the information hungrily.

The horse found the boy, who needed him again. He was lying on the ground of the forest, unconscious because the old lady had beaten the knife until there was no sign of iron left. (She had proceeded to kidnap the goddess, no longer fearing pursuit.) The boy's heart still beat, however, because the ogress had been unable to break the knife. The horse took him back to the mountaintop realm and then raced off to find his three long-lost friends.

Early in the morning, the horse arrived at their camp and lay down his head. The three men were shocked to see him. "Where did you come from?" they asked. "Where's our friend?" They leaped onto their horses. "Just show us the way!"

Up the mountain trail the horse led them, and they panicked when they found their friend comatose. They called out to him to no avail.

Finally they did a prophecy through which they discovered how the ogress had hurt him by bludgeoning his knife.

Fortunately, the careless woman had tossed the disfigured knife onto the palace floor. The three men took the knife to have it fixed, refinished with gold and silver. As it was hammered back into shape, the boy awoke as if from a long sleep. Before he had time to yawn and stretch, he was barraged with questions. "How come you're king of this place?" "Why did you leave us?" "What happened?"

Still rather dazed, he responded as best he could. "Well, I was just listening to my horse. He told me to come ahead…and I won the goddess, and I've been enjoying life up here…but I missed you guys, and I searched for you all the time—I just couldn't find you anywhere!"

They did not have time to delve very deeply into the matter, however, because the boy soon realized that the old lady had kidnapped his wife. "We must get her back!" he exclaimed.

The four men raced to the Western Kingdom. There, a great celebration was taking place. People sang and danced, playing sports and shooting arrows. The prince stood in wedding attire near his parents, and the ogress also stood nearby, gloating at the thought of her great wealth. The goddess looked desolately into the crowd, dreading the coming marriage. Once or twice, she thought she spied her husband, but she knew that it could not be him, for he was with a group of people she had never seen before.

"Your majesty," the hunter cried out with his booming voice. "We are travelers from the region beyond. May we join your party and show off our skills?"

"Of course!" said the king. "This is a time for showing off skills."

The hunter stepped forward, placing four sturdy arrows in his bow. He aimed toward the target at which other archers had been shooting, but in a split-second, he changed direction as the arrows flew. They sailed smoothly in the air, and then—poom!—poom!—poom!—poom! King, queen, prince, and old lady collapsed with arrows in their hearts!

Lake-drinker spit out a lake, and they threw the dead bodies in.

Hill-lifter placed a hill over the lake so that their spirits could never escape to haunt the his friends. The goddess and her boy had a happy reunion, and realized that they and their companions could now have the Western Kingdom as well.

With a victorious laugh, the old man came to his tale's end.
"I wonder why he decided to tell us that story," I said.
"Who knows? Who knows which way his marbles will roll once he starts talking?" Sara mused.

XVI. Rain and Rebirth

One day at the Pyramid as Namrata and I were finishing dinner, it started raining. Like Teatime and nearly all the other restaurants on the street, the entrance walls were open, so we could see it around us, the sound of the rain pleasant as it hit the roof. As we were paying the bill, there was a sudden downpour, the water breaking from the sky the way it had on our boating trip.

Namrata groaned that she had a white shirt on. "It's going to become transparent!"

"It's light—it'll be okay," I replied calmly. The waiter kindly asked if he should hail us a taxi, but the hotel was just down the street...

I had been eating the plainest food available at the restaurant, feeling only half-awake to life as I usually did during my time in Nepal. This day fell between my bedridden state and my two extra days off from interviewing; I was still suffering from the stomach bug, and it combined with my breathing trouble to make me especially pathetic.

But the rain brought my spirit to life again. It *was* a comparatively "light" rain as I had said, but monsoon rain comes down in huge, heavy drops even when it is sparse. It made me deliriously happy as it thundered down. "Namrata, it's so great!" I laughed, as we ran around the corner. Unfortunately for her, the rain grew heavier as we splashed down the street. She ran huddled over, her arms across her chest. "Your back's starting to show through!" I informed, moving behind her. "Don't worry—I'll cover you. But you have to promise to put on a raincoat and come back out with me! This is great!"

When we reached our room, by this time on the first floor instead of the third where we had stayed at first. I slipped into my red raincoat and picked up my bedraggled umbrella. Namrata ripped off her sopping shirt and put on her coat, which had a hood, joining me as I ran back out.

I usually did not like monsoon rain in the city areas as much as in less populated, cleaner areas. Plodding through the flooded streets of Lakeside in open-toed monsoon *chapals* becomes a chore as the water, mixing with spit and cow dung and far dirtier trash from the streets, soaks into the feet. Cities pollute the rain. But on this day, I was madly exuberant, laughing with Namrata as the rain struck us and we walked along the main street, trying to stay on dry areas. At this point, the dryer places were islands. So much water everywhere, the flooded roads in some places knee-deep.

The stores on each side were raised above the street. We passed the Kashmiri papier maché shops, Tibetan shops filled with jewelry or *thanka* paintings, clothing shops with bright wrap-around skirts in "Indian" prints. We passed the bookstore where I enjoyed browsing through the English section. Books on "spirituality" were hot with tourists, and there were many illustrated copies of the *Kama Sutra*.

I remember standing for a long while halfway down the main street as the rain hit my umbrella until Namrata was ready to return. The intersection beside Brad and Sara's hotel had turned into a river with a strong current, our own flooded street almost pitch-black as we pushed our way to Lake Palace. I complained about having to wade home by myself one night when it was like this. "Waaaaaade in the waaaaater…" Namrata started singing. She did that every time I mentioned wading in water, but she did not remember the rest of the lyrics. I taught her as we forged our way back.

Like the rain and sun and all the other uncontrollable elements that affect human life, uncanny coincidences scream at people to examine them for deeper meaning. One such synchronicity was how room number 303 followed us through our travels. It first surfaced at Pema Lamo, where our room with its pink bathroom and green carpet was number three on the third floor. I remembered off-handedly how it was my room number during my first year of college and then did not think of it again until we reached the forsaken hotel in Pokhara, where our room number was the same. Then at Lake Palace, the first room they showed us was 303, though they put us in the room across from it when we came back, telling us that they had promised it to someone else (but we suspect it was because we had negotiated lower rates). To clinch the recurrence of the number, Namrata and I balked when we saw it above the room the receptionist was opening for us at a hotel in Katmandu where we stayed for a night before I left Nepal.

Did we believe it meant something? Do you believe it means something? Perhaps a type of karmic tease, some real-life symbolism? Some people consider examining patterns like this one irrational. Others will insist empathically that some sort of meaning lies in the event. What makes a belief rational or irrational? And what difference does tradition make? The same people who would be understanding if a Nepali believed in spirits may mock a New Ager in the US for believing. Namrata and I did yoga every morning at Pema Lamo but mocked the Westerners on the roof across from us where they would gather each morning, stretching and beating drums in an effort to be one with the monks around them. Where exactly does inauthenticity lie? Isn't tradition somewhat inauthentic too?

Namrata and I were told once or twice that the belief of reincarnation instilled in the general Nepali population is the reason for the stability of its people—that they know, even if they die, there will always be chances, that life as we know it does not really end with death.

There are other sides to this belief as well. When people die, many Nepalis don't let them go; they build small *stupas* near their houses, praying every year to the soul of the departed. Bad spirits, we were told, sometimes play mischief because until they are reborn, they stay nearby.

There is a female shaman who knows about these things. People wait in long lines for her to tell them whether their fathers or sisters or uncles-in-law are ghosts or reborn or on other planets. Namrata and I were fascinated to hear of her, and given time, thought we might try and look her up when we were in Katmandu again.

When we were in Katmandu again, I had the best shopping experience of all my time in Nepal. I had just changed my ticket for an early return at the Royal Nepal Airlines office with no hassle or cost. It was raining lightly and I wrapped my *dupata* around my head, picking up some almonds because Namrata was so hungry she thought she would faint and there were no restaurants immediately in sight. I fell in love with almonds in my time in Nepal, where they replaced cashews as my favorite nuts. I carried them everywhere: to munch on during excursions, to share with Namrata, Brad, and Sara, to hand to beggars in the place of money.

Almonds in hand to tide us over, I paused at the window of a jewelry store. Namrata had wanted to buy gifts for her family and friends, and so I joined her in doing the same. By now, scanning store windows was a habit. The entrance of this one was blocked by men doing construction work, but the shopkeeper saw us and heartily encouraged us to come in.

What I liked most about the place was that the owner seemed so genuine. He chatted with us pleasantly and instructed his son, a glasses-clad boy of nine or ten, to sell us the jewelry. The boy, who was shy, did not make a flamboyant presentation of the treasures at hand. When we wondered how much a tiger eye ring or a string of amethyst cost, he would look to his father and ask before turning to tell us. If he managed to sell us something, his father told him, he would have his commission in his drink of choice.

I selected a garnet necklace for my sister, the beads smooth and oval. The shop owner cut a fresh strand from the coil of them under the glass and attached a clasp. Namrata picked a necklace as well. The owner offered Namrata and me tea or cold drinks, and I chose *lychee* juice like his son, who ran off to buy them. The wife and daughter of the owner walked in, and he introduced them briefly before they wandered into the back of the store.

The *lychee* juice was cold and sweet and tasted just like the fruit. The *lychee* is one of the fruits I can eat fresh only when I visit India, except once in a long while when my family tests the imported *lychees* at a farmer's market. At Lakeside, the only fruits that were available during the monsoon were mangoes, pineapples and bananas.

XVII. The Younger Shaman

The shaman-deity needed proximity in order to make a better diagnosis. At first, when he beckoned for me to come nearer, the translator simply told me to perch on another bed that was closer to him, which relieved me slightly because I was not overly anxious to get too close. But as he wished to delve further into my ailments, six feet away proved too far. He beckoned to the chair in front of him, and reluctantly, I walked up to him and sat...

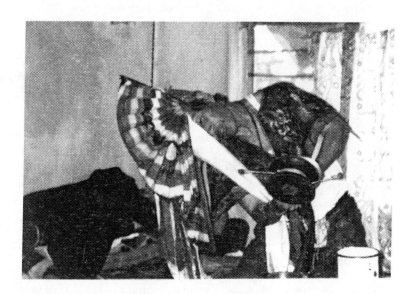

The first time I experienced a shamanic healing *puja*, I was the patient. Our translator made an appointment for us, and on the day it was scheduled, I woke up in a much better mood than I had been in the day before. My head still throbbed, and my stomach was not quite right yet, but Namrata and I were no longer bedridden with fevers.

I had suggested noon rather than eleven o'clock as our interview time for the day, so we did not have to meet Sara and Brad for breakfast until eleven. I had an ulterior motive: at ten, I watched *Farscape* on television, ecstatic to see my favorite show for an entire hour without the power going out in the middle. Namrata went ahead to Teatime at ten to eleven; I strutted out after my show was over and laughed as I saw Sara and Brad trailing across the street in front of me, late for breakfast as well.

"Live the life you love, love the life you live" is the slogan on the wall in the restaurant. Our usual waiter was skinny and shy, exceedingly polite. "Yes, please?" he would say as we gave him our orders in the morning. "Yes, please, thank you," he replied once before heading back to the kitchen with our requests.

This morning, I did not want my regular banana "crepe," which was more of a *dosa*. The banana, I feared, or the oil might hurt my stomach. "Can I have some plain rice?" I asked the waiter. He brought it to me in a large steel bowl, and I was content to chew as dryly as I could.

When we reached the camp, Namrata, Brad, Sara and I followed our translator to the abode of the camp's younger shaman. One of Ngodup's little boys came to watch as well. Our translator introduced us to the shaman and his brother-in-law. Both men smiled at us genially. The shaman's words might become a bit obscure when he was possessed by a deity, Ngodup explained, so the brother-in-law would translate the old Tibetan dialect.

Most of the light in the dim, rectangular room came from the windows: one behind the shaman and two windows in the wall to his left. A bed lined the walls on each side of the room. The shaman sat on his bed beside his altar, and we spread out on the others. Namrata and I sat on the bed beside the entrance, on the opposite side of the room from the shaman.

I did not know entirely what a healing *puja* entailed. Our translator had promised a diagnosing forecast, had described some of the healings he had witnessed at the camp. Once, he insisted, the shaman cured his rabies when a mad dog bit him. Another time, his wife's gall stones were dissolved by a shaman. Tibetan shamans, he told me, are far more powerful than Nepali shamans.

To a large extent, Ngodup's belief pushed me into the realm of credulous uncertainty that I entered as I listened to the other shaman's story of his grandfather's healing. So when I sat before the shaman as he chanted, I was quite willing to believe unless I had cause to disbelieve. I sat hoping for a taste of what Ngodup had promised.

As the shaman chanted himself into a trance with his drum and bell, we were observers. We were present, but we were separate from him. Curious outsiders. When I first saw him going into spasms, leaping up and dancing, I found it unnerving, but he calmed down and settled on the bed. He thought he saw where we come from. "It is early morning there."

It would have been, though I could not make sense of what he said next. He asked if my house was five or six stories high with yellowish ivory paint. I was trying to make his words make sense. After all, why he would speak of a house if he didn't truly believe he saw it? The five- or six-story-high house I could not picture unless he spoke of our hotel. (Also trying to make it work, Sara questioned whether the place could be somewhere I lived in past years, perhaps a dorm—or maybe someplace in London?)

I seemed to have some difficulty breathing, he said. This was true. I wondered vaguely if the translator might have hinted at it— although how he could have known I don't know.

That was when the shaman—diety—called me to sit in the wooden chair in front of him, and I wonder how hesitant I looked as I stepped six feet forward. Being so close to his powerful presence unsettled me. His energy full and strong, he took my wrist and felt my pulses. As with Dr. Cheokyi, this action informed him that there was something wrong with my stomach. He said something else.

Without warning, the brother-in-law started unbuttoning my shirt. I was taken aback but determined to stay calm. Ngodup came up behind me to explain what was going on, which put me more at ease. A red netted cloth was placed on my stomach.

I was already growing nervous as the deity-reflection opened his mouth once or twice, his red tongue lapping out. I remembered what Ngodup had told us about shamans' simply sucking the illness out of patients, the diseases manifesting as inch-long insects or other bizarre things.

But it was still a shock when he suddenly lunged forward, sucking my stomach for an instant in a sloppy open-mouthed kiss. I can't remember whether or not I shrieked. The cloth whipped away, caught in his teeth. Above it, his eyes were huge.

He took the cloth away in his hands, spitting into the white porcelain dish on the stand beside him. Namrata ran up behind me and gave me a hug. I was soothed by her presence. A small brown stone sat in the dish. "He says it is your gall stone," Ngodup told me.

The deity-in-the-shaman's-body reached forward with the red netting. "Again?" I groaned, slightly distraught as he placed it on a different spot on my stomach. He sucked it off again, and this time, a long black insect-like thing that Ngodup called a pupa sat in the porcelain dish. This, the deity-shaman told me, was the manifestation of whatever was wrong with my spleen. The gallstone I could take with me to show my doctors, but the pupa was for him. He took the black thing out of the dish and ate it.

The deity-reflection asked if Namrata wanted him to perform a forecast for her. She said no.

He chanted himself out of the trance, and then the shaman smiled at me with his usual eyes and asked what had happened in the *puja*.

I was determined to keep the gall stone. Namrata showed it to someone in our hotel who said that the consistency was the same as his sister's gall stone but did not believe it could be mine. Sara wanted me to have DNA testing done on the stone. Brad remained certain that the brother-in-law must have brought in a rock from the street, and Namrata, who admittedly laughed through the healing, refused to believe that the stone could have come from me even if the DNA matched because it would shake her beliefs too soundly. Regardless of opinion, the small stone, wrapped in black plastic, sat in my purse until I came home and lost track of it. Sara could kill me.

After the healing *puja*, we went back to Ngodup's house, where Namrata and I had hot lemons and Sara and Brad had tea. My drink was tart and soothing as it slipped down my throat.

Before going, we followed him outside the house to watch my hemp paper being made. Ngodup was in the hemp business, experimenting with shirts, sandals, skirts made with the strong material. I had purchased six sheets of pure hemp paper for my paintings, and workers were placing the treated plant on some sort of canvas to dry. I was weary of the dog chained up outside beside the men; it growled ferociously, biting toward us. Brad befriended it.

That night, I wrote to my friends and family in detail about my shamanic encounter:

you know how you're supposed to have unsettling experiences while you travel? well, up until this point, i haven't had any at all. and then i lived through today. okay, that sounds really dramatic, but so was my experience. mainly because it was rather freaky...

We went to a dinner-and-movie restaurant, one of many that lined the streets of Lakeside. I don't remember which movie was playing. We decided to take the next day off.

(The following section is based on what the shaman told me of his experience when he heals people. Most of it was written as I observed a *puja*, trying to get into his head even as I noted what was going on externally.)

The camp's younger shaman shakes his drum with one hand, a bell clanging in the other as he chants his trance-like song, entering into different phases of consciousness. He stops singing to sip his tea, asking after the old man who he will cure first, a Nepali with infected vocal cords. Faster and louder, he beats, singing with greater intensity, his eyes squeezing shut and then opening momentarily in a focused glare—looking at what? His body is tense now, voice trembling along with his arms as they shake the drum and his head as he rocks.

Namrata, Sara, and I sit on the bed to the shaman's left. We examine the family that has come for the healing *puja*. Across from us, the old man with the infected vocal cords lies waiting. He is the head of a family, and he has married his cousin (our translator explains when he comes back into the room). His son, born in a line of cousins marrying cousins, has only eight fingers, his hands forming V's where his middle fingers should be. His wife and sister flank him; they are waiting to be healed as well. Three children are also present, a little boy who sits on his mother's lap and two little girls who look over a book, practicing their English and singing *"Kuch Kuch Hota Hai."*

When we entered the room, the shaman was already well into the initial stage of his chanting, entering his first trance. Now he stops to pull out the garments he will wear when the deity enters, starting the drum and bell again with a new intensity, eyes closing, half-opening, closing. In his mind, mirrors reveal themselves, flashing into existence like TV screens. Enormous people decked in ornaments, huge and bright, are glimpsed by his mind's eye. He is in the second phase of his trance, in a smoky realm surrounded by faded rainbows. To focus on a deity, he must concentrate.

Half-conscious, he sees us as flames that emanate from our foreheads, stars in the middle of our faces.

He beats the drum furiously now; the bell clangs with fervor. His voice takes on a new, sharper tone. Louder, louder, faster, faster…the drum goes on beating as the voice and the bell stop…and then he puts it down, donning his garments…

Singing again, he holds out his hat with its spectrum of colors and mirrors, like a transistor. The gods reveal themselves to him, flashing like rays of lightning. He focuses on the reflection of a deity as he chants.

And then the hat goes on, allowing the chanter to become the reflection. The drum starts beating once again, the rest of his body stable, his eyes averted. The bell is lifted as well, and bell and drum create an uncanny rhythm before settling down to a beat he can sing to. Now and then, the bell pauses, allowing the drum to render a powerful moment in its thumping solo.

He lifts something from the altar, the altar of Padmasanbhawa where his brother-in-law lit two candles before the *puja* started. Rice, water, milk, and tea sit around the lighted candles in four bowls of— copper? Steel? In the shadowed candlelight I cannot tell. The contents are offerings, each to a different realm of beings: milk is for the lizard-like *nags* and *naginis*; tea signifies blood, an offering to the wrathful deities; water…what does water signify? I can no longer make out the translator's whispered response.

What he has lifted from the altar is a *vajra*, a ritual object symbolizing indestructibility. With it, he scatters rice, presents to deities who cure. The rice is also offered to bad spirits, who are told to be satisfied with the grains and stop their harm. Our translator explains that for an extremely powerful shaman, a simple meditation is enough; the less powerful you are, the more grains you must offer. "May this offering make your body strong, your speech exact, your heart peaceful," the traditional incantation declares.

The bell has stopped altogether now, the *vajra* in his hand taking on a new significance as he sing-chants, praying…

The drum shakes, the bell shakes, his head shakes. The brother-in-law perches on the bed with Namrata and me, tossing rice into the air. It scatters across the floor. Furiously, the bell shakes, the drum shakes, his head shakes. A steely glare moves around the room, meeting thirteen foreheads of flame on four beds.

Suddenly, legs are shaking along with bell and drum as he dances on the floor. Knees jerk feet abruptly from side to side. He jumps onto the bed, legs, arms, head shaking. Colors adorn him, his hat a rainbow, colorful breastcloth and apron covering his usual banyan and pants. European tourists who came in to observe the *puja* take a photograph.

And now, the loud, authoritative voice so different from the good-humored sound that usually emanates from the small man beckons the first patient. The hoarse-throated man steps forward, sitting on a chair before the shaman who is no longer the shaman. The deity questions him demandingly. Upon hearing an answer, he goes into a tirade, screaming the reason that the man contracted his illness. He accuses him of having a dull mind, saying that his psyche does not possess the capacity to feel more than one emotion at a time. "He gets angry and feels nothing else," the translator explains, "speaking too loudly for too long." Ninety days ago, the shaman-deity goes on, through a door between two doors, the man ate a mid-day meal that gave him a cold. The Nepali people in the room appear to agree.

The old man has screamed his voice away, but the deity prepares himself to bring it back, singing once again, perhaps changing to the reflection of a deity more appropriate for the task at hand. The brother-in-law removes strings of beads from the old man's shriveled neck. He places the red netting-cloth with which I am intimately familiar on his throat, bell cupping the old man's mouth for a moment as the shaman-deity prepares himself, inching closer and closer.

And then he launches himself onto him, sucking with a great slurp, the net coming away with his mouth as he draws back as quickly as he came. The brother-in-law pours water into a white porcelain bowl, and a fluid is spit out by the shaman-deity, floating vilely for the curious onlookers who have now come closer and are peering at it. But his job is not finished; before moving on to the next patient, he has yet to suck more fluid and two large insect-like creatures from the man. Again, again, again he sucks.

The next patient, a woman in the conventionally incestuous family, had problems with the snake-like *nags* according to the shaman.

The red cloth reappears, and he sucks her neck like a vampire, spitting something ambiguous out for the crowd to see in the dim room. Then the red cloth moves to her upper cheek, and once again, something I cannot see is spit out. The lady, it seems, smoked too many cigarettes.

Then the wife of the four-fingered man approaches, and the shaman-deity shoos her little boy back. Clothing pulls apart to reveal a stomach; some sort of juice is sucked out, the manifestation of what disease we will never know because now our translator is one with the family members, crowding around to look.

But this woman also suffers from epilepsy, as our translator explains for a moment, coming back to us. Although it sounds not like epilepsy, exactly; in essence, she suffers fainting spells. The cloth is placed on her head, and the bell and drum sound once again. A *yeti* is called, the deity best at dealing with epileptics, and it cannot look directly at any of us. Being a gorilla, it fears the flames that human beings manifest themselves as to those of the godly realm. Eyes averted, it reaches out, long copper-nailed fingers in blunt disguise, and grabs the cloth with its hands from the woman's head. The healing is over.

During the height of my observations, as I was writing madly, trying to merge what I had just learned about the specifics of the shaman's experiences and practices with what I was seeing, my pen slipped under the bed. I fished around madly for quite a while as Sara and Namrata told me to forget about it and pay attention, as frustrated as a writer can be when consciousness is flowing in perfect harmony with her surroundings but her means of expression is lost.

It takes a much shorter time for him to come out of a trance than it does to enter one. Each of the offerings is discarded outside, except the rice, which he sprinkles about the floor. He looks exhausted afterwards, but good-humored once again as he asks us in his normal voice what he did; once the deity has control, he loses consciousness. In order to be cured of suffering, we must keep our souls as pure as snow, he tells us. He knows from experience.

The *puja* lasted for about an hour. The rain meets us as we come out, falling harder and harder, the earlier promise of a sunny day revoked. Namrata and Sara groan pitifully, and I smile as I watch it come down, hearing the large splattering sound of drops hitting rooftops.

The young shaman was born in Tibet before the Chinese occupation. He remembers the day that he went to see the black-necked cranes. It was his thirteenth winter, and the sun was cold. There was a river that became a lake before snaking off as a river again. There, two cranes danced elegantly. Nearby, two vultures showed off their wings.

His parents berated him upon his description of the scene when he returned home. "Your evil eye must have seen them! It's winter; there are no cranes."

And yet he saw things. Illusions beckoned all around him, pulling him into their world. He saw gods, and he saw devils. He could not mention them to others without them turning away unbelieving ears and telling him to be silent.

Once he was lost for three days. His family requested a *lama* to prophesy where he was, and they discovered that he was destined to be a shaman. "Don't worry when he gets lost," the *lama* told them. "He is simply in another realm."

So they did not worry when he was lost a second time, leaving them for eight days. When he returned home from these journeys, he felt as though he had awakened from a deep sleep. Vague recollections of walking through fields of grain, past blooming flowers, remained. The *lama* told him not to expect anything from his visions and not to feel that they would harm him. "Just enjoy the scenery," he said. So the boy smiled in bliss when he saw girls adorned in beautiful ornaments riding horses past him. He shrank away when formless creatures, all eyes and no body, slithered his way, trying not to fear them. By the time he was twenty-five, he was able to control his visions because of the training of his guru.

And then his powers came in a blast, and the visions drove him mad. He was connecting, without intending to, without wanting to, with supernatural forces. All the time now and not in spurts like before.

He cannot remember everything from this time, but to rescue him from his madness, his teacher told him that he had to begin his life as a shaman. Otherwise, the visions would drive him irreparably insane. The guru gave him a special blessing to clarify his veins, his arteries, his nerves.

Many *Rinpoches*, meditation masters, taught him. His visions were cleared by the special blessings and consecrations of *lamas* who purified his powers. After a time, he began to feel more confident in his abilities, wearing the hat with pride instead of hesitation.

Shamans find it difficult to come to power in the presence of others who are in tune with the gods. In the presence of other shamans, for instance, the less powerful shamans are said to quiver before the emanations from their stronger counterparts. When my shaman was 50, he had difficulty asking a deity to enter in a monastery as a high-ranking *lama* judged him. *Maybe the deities will not come this time*, he feared, as he tried to enter a trance, the *lama* waiting before him. But he succeeded, regaining confidence in his abilities. He says he is very happy now.

As he told us, the shaman tries to do no harm, to do what he can to help, and to be social. As all shamans are, he is especially renowned for treating anthrax, epilepsy, and rabies. Eight hundred medicine gods exist, but usually, the reflection of Thangla, a very powerful and effective deity, enters. Particular deities specialize in only one or two diseases; epilepsy, for instance, can be successfully cured by the bird-god Garuda or Tarku Tanoksokar, a wrathful *yeti*. He remembers a monk who had become thin because of his cough. The patient's lung was stuck to his ribs, and the Western doctor insisted upon an operation. After the deity entered, it sucked out a blood clot; the monk and his guru grew very happy at the successful results.

He sees spirits. Four months ago, he walked into a group of naked people. He recognized a relative of his who had died six or seven years before. "Oh, Uncle, you're here," he said to the shaman.

"Why are you here—you're dead!" the shaman realized and then chanted the traditional prayer asking for the release of suffering from all living beings: "*Om ma né pad mé hoong...*"

"Thank you," said his naked nephew and disappeared.

He has mistreated deities. For a time, the shaman succumbed to greed, charging patients when he performed *pujas* rather than waiting until they were cured and allowing them to pay as they wished. Rising in anger, high-ranking deities haunted his dreams. They called him "Promise-breaker," appalled that he was selling them.

For ten days, he was driven into madness. He did not describe in detail his experience of this time, but the visions he saw threw his mind into a state of turmoil. He suffered physically as well as mentally. Stricken with tuberculosis, he agonized for two years before regaining health.

During his struggle with the punishing deities, he turned to alcohol, drinking heavily to forget his distress. But intoxication only accentuated his pain and helplessness, pulling him deeper into madness as gods inflicted their retribution.

The shaman never asks anything of patients now. He trusts, as the deities told him, that if the patients are cured, they will give what they can.

"How old are you, sister?" the shaman asks me in English while the translator takes a break.

"Twenty-one," I answer.

"Thirty-one?"

"No, *twenty*-one."

Namrata and Sara each answer "twenty" under his questioning gaze. He tells us that he is fifty-nine, and we reply that he doesn't look it. His hair is very black, his features smooth as a forty-year-old's.

"Are you afraid of snakes?" he asks Sara. (He is speaking in Tibetan again. Our translator has returned.)

She is rather confused by the sudden question, but I point to Namrata as having a definite phobia thanks to the time that she was nearly attacked by two of them.

"This next year will be Year of the Dragon," the shaman says. "You should watch out for snakes." Black snakes, green snakes that are very poisonous… Our translator describes how he used to be the resident snake-catcher, using a long bundle with string to coil up and throw...

Laughing, the shaman relates the story of a Swiss volunteer named Shrueberger, or something like that. He had lived for a while in the camp years ago, and snake collecting was his passion. One day, he caught a sausage-like snake that lay sluggish and inactive in his home. It was large and bulky, and he could not tell its tail from its head. In the late evening, when his interpreter Sherpa came home, he told him to come and help him identify his snake. The Swiss man picked up the lethargic creature, then felt a stab of pain as it suddenly bit him.

He sucked his blood, spitting out the venom, but he felt an odd sensation coming over him. Looking at his book of snakes, he identified the snake as deadly poisonous and knew he would die. "I have been killed by a snake," he had time to write before he collapsed for good. "No one is responsible for my death."

His last note signed, the Swiss man lay dead with ninety snakes writhing in the room. No one dared to enter.

XVIII. Night

Craving solitude, I make my way to the roof of Lake Palace as the lights black out and reappear haphazardly. As I find whenever I visit India, privacy in Nepal is rare, and I feel the strains of always being watched. Here, I can escape it all for a bit.

Half the roof is the enormous terrace on the sixth story, where the best room of the hotel is located; to the side of the terrace, steps lead to the second half, the roof of the master room. On top, a *stupa* gazes out with large painted eyes, a small temple that cannot fit more than two, three people.

I stand on the sixth floor terrace, looking toward the lake. When the electricity is on, lights glitter below and roll up the sides of the surrounding hills. Mist sometimes obscures the elusive *stupa* on the hill beside the lake, which is also alight. Guests awake in The Hotel Stupa next door (which, ironically, has no *stupa* on its roof), appear through windows in miniature dollhouse scenes. Sheathed in darkness and towering above most of Lakeside, I feel inconspicuous enough to let down my reserve.

I don't know what it is that makes me so afraid of discovery, but every time I think I hear footsteps traipsing up the stairs, I freeze, examining the doors to ensure that no one will discover me doing anything other than standing granite-still, gazing blandly into the distance. I was not so self-conscious the first time I came up, dragging Namrata along; we explored the roof, visiting the small *stupa* on top, spinning about wildly. Namrata tried to teach me how to belly dance. But there's something different about ignoring intrusion when your attention is occupied by another person from ignoring onlookers when your eyes are on yourself, in your own mind, allowing yourself to be. The latter, to me, is an intimate experience, and I am very weary of someone's slipping onto the roof and spying on me.

But no one comes. I waltz across the terrace tiles to my heart's content, old melodies from long ago resurfacing haphazardly in my mind. I sing softly, listening to the calls of salamanders. Then, stopping to meditate, I breathe in deeply, the night air above as diesel-free as Lakeside can get.

Afterward

by Namrata Shah

As our six week stay in Nepal dwindled to an end, Shilpa and I treated ourselves to a whitewater rafting trip along the Trisuli River. Shilpa awoke that day with a sprained neck and despite my suggestions to stay home and relax, she insisted on going rafting. The three Himalayan ranges, usually not visible during the cloudy monsoon season, stood tall and majestic on our last day in Pokhara. Their overwhelming presence filled the sky and I remember thinking that I had seen nothing so perfect and so powerful.

If for nothing else our guide was worth getting up for at six in the morning. *Charisma* is the word that comes to mind when I describe him. But it was undeniably his well-built muscular stature—allowing him to steer our raft with ease—which caught my attention. His energy was refreshing. If possible I would have taken him to the States with me!

Now about the rest of the crew… A sweet-looking Japanese husband and wife, the adventurous German couple and the two Indian men, who kept complaining about not receiving breakfast on this trip. "Mr. India"—as our guide called him—hardly put forth any effort while paddling and later complained about his not-so-chilled can of Coke. Despite his eccentricities, we all managed to enjoy our time together. Our guide started a water fight—as an icebreaker I suppose—by first splashing Shilpa with his paddle. Some of the crewmembers even resorted to throwing full buckets of water at each other. Sweating in the scorching summer heat, we were thankful for having the water fight.

Our guide was a flirt. During lunchtime he handed Shilpa and me a bucket each. We were to follow him to a nearby waterfall and retrieve water for drinking purposes (iodized of course!). After having filled his bucket our guide turned toward us with a smirk on his face and in a thick Nepali accent said, "You do like this." *Splash*. Shilpa immediately retaliated with her own splurge of water while I, unprepared for the spontaneity, stood sopping wet and took some time to fill my bucket with water. Thus started our short-lived but entertaining water fight.

We headed back with our buckets full of water for lunchtime. But lunch could hardly be called a lunch for me. I was afraid that the iodine had not completely killed all the germs in the veggies. I thus stuck with my peanut butter and jelly sandwich while the rest of the crew ate a hearty lunch. Grrrh…

Our rafting trip ended and some of the crew headed toward a nearby waterfall for a "shower." With our eyes, Shilpa and I traced the waterfall to its source where the water looked unstoppable. And we—well, mostly Shilpa, who always gets me into trouble (the sprained ankle being a prime example)—decided to head up. We ascended carefully for I was in no mood for another sprain. Once at the top, I immersed myself in the water while maintaining a steady balance. As I held on to any frictional force the water had not managed to swallow up, the pouring water transmitted energy into me. For whatever reason, maybe it was because I had not showered in the past few days, I felt a feeling of satisfaction.

Satisfaction is a very unfamiliar feeling to me. Unlike Shilpa, I don't feel the need to be satisfied in order to be happy. I'm happiest when I am busy, but never satisfied. There is always something more I can achieve. Paradoxically, I usually do things just for the thrill of them and not for the end goal. There is no end goal for me. While we were in Nepal, I was never satisfied with our research. There was always something I failed to comprehend. I felt distanced from the culture. Because of this I could not internalize how the patients felt.

I remember sitting in the Younger Shaman's house, bewildered by my surroundings. We were about to witness a shamanic healing ceremony. The Shaman—possessed by the incarnation of Medicine Buddha—was in a trance, dancing and drumming wildly while adorned in his paraphernalia. All this was in preparation for curing his "patients." I was astonished to find so many Nepalis going to a Shaman with an illness rather than an allopathic physician in a nearby hospital. Being raised in a strictly allopathic background, relating to any alternative healing methods was difficult for me. I had pursued my research endeavor with a clear distinction between the "norm," allopathic medicine and the "other," alternative medicine. This mindset allowed me to view my surroundings with a distance. But there were times when that distance deteriorated and I found myself wanting to forcefully direct the Shaman's patients to an allopathic hospital, afraid that they would miss an opportunity to heal in the early stages of their sickness. Allopathic medicine was the only method of healing I was familiar with and the only method I knew to work.

I noticed a distinction between the way Western and Nepali healers interacted with their patients. The doctors in Nepal seemed unafraid of getting close to their patients. It might just be a cultural thing; I'm not sure. In Western society, we admire the distance between patients and physicians. I took this distance for granted; if a physician was emotionally involved with a patient, her judgments about the treatment would be biased. Now, I don't think the distance is necessary for treatment to be effective, and I question this standard.

Achievement comes to me in retrospect. I am satisfied with our research now; I learned something new, it was a good time... More than anything I learned to think beyond my thoughts.